NAHUM

Julia Myers O'Brien

SHEFFIELD ACADEMIC PRESS
A Continuum imprint
LONDON • NEW YORK

Readings: A New Biblical Commentary

General Editor
John Jarick

N A H U M

Published by
Sheffield Academic Press Ltd
The Tower Building, 11 York Road, London SE1 7NX
370 Lexington Avenue, New York, NY 10017-6550

www.SheffieldAcademicPress.com
www.continuumbooks.com

British Library Cataloguing-in-Publication Data

A catalogue record for this book is available from the British Library

Typeset by Sheffield Academic Press
Printed on acid-free paper in Great Britain by Bookcraft Ltd, Midsomer Norton, Bath

ISBN   1-84127-299-X (hardback)
        1-84127-300-7 (paperback)

A Dedication

Dear Anna,

This book is written with your face before me. Literally, as I work on it, you and I eat dinner and do homework and make life. You are in my presence as I write. But, as importantly to me, your presence informs all that I do. I write and I teach with one primary question: how might my interpretive practices help shape a world in which you—and all people—might flourish? As you grow into naming and wrestling your own questions, may you find blessings for yourself and for others.

Your mother

Contents

List of Illustrations

Acknowledgments

I am grateful to the friends who have stuck with me through my wrestling with Nahum. Greg Carey, Philip Davies, Garry Walton, Kharma Amos, and Peter Eaton have been gracious and helpful readers, on issues substantive and stylistic. The students in two terms of my 'Prophets of Divine Wrath' class at Lancaster Theological Seminary in Lancaster, PA, sat with me in the discomfort of Nahum and taught me much about reading the Bible and about the ways in which violence shapes our imaginations and our lives. Anabel, Greg, Peter, Judy Siker, and Bart Ehrman have listened and been my friends, and to them I am grateful. My sincere thanks goes to John Jarick for being a kind and patient editor.

Abbreviations

AB	*Anchor Bible*
ABD	David Noel Freedman (ed.), *The Anchor Bible Dictionary* (New York: Doubleday, 1992)
ASV	American Standard Version
BHS	*Biblia hebraica stuttgartensia*
BibInt	*Biblical Interpretation: A Journal of Contemporary Approaches*
BibOr	Biblica et orientalia
BibSem	The Biblical Seminar
BZAW	*Beihefte zur Zeitschrift für die Alttestamentliche Wissenschaft*
CBQ	*Catholic Biblical Quarterly*
ConBOT	Coniectanea biblica, Old Testament
DBI	*Dictionary of Biblical Interpretation* (ed. J.H. Hayes; 2 vols.; Nashville: Abingdon Press)
EncJud	*Encyclopaedia Judaica*
FCB	Feminist Companion to the Bible
FOTL	Forms of Old Testament Literature
GTJ	*Grace Theological Journal*
HB	Hebrew Bible
HBC	*Harper's Bible Commentary* (ed. J.L. Mays; San Francisco: Harper & Row, 1988)
HUCA	*Hebrew Union College Annual*
IB	*Interpreter's Bible*
IBS	*Irish Biblical Studies*
ICC	International Critical Commentary
ITC	International Theological Commentary
JBL	*Journal of Biblical Literature*
JETS	*Journal of the Evangelical Theological Society*
JSOT	*Journal of the Study of the Old Testament*
JSOTSup	*Journal of the Study of the Old Testament*, Supplement Series
KJV	King James Version
NAB	New American Bible
NASB	New American Standard Bible
NIB	*New Interpreter's Bible* (ed. L.E. Keck; 12 vols.; Nashville: Abingdon, 1994)
NIV	New International Version
NJB	New Jerusalem Bible

NKJV	New King James Version
NRSV	New Revised Standard Version
OTE	*Old Testament Essays*
OTG	Old Testament Guides
OTL	Old Testament Library
OTS	*Oudtestamentlische Studiën*
PmB	*The Postmodern Bible* (The Bible and Culture Collective; New Haven: Yale University Press, 1995)
RSV	Revised Standard Version
SBL	Society of Biblical Literature
SBLDS	SBL Dissertation Series
VT	*Vetus Testamentum*
VTSup	*Vetus Testamentum*, Supplements
WBC	Word Biblical Commentary
ZAW	*Zeitschrift für die alttestamentliche Wissenschaft*

Introduction

I find the invitation to read Nahum from a literary perspective both a delight and a challenge. The task is a delight because the book is so rich in literary features. Through the use of assonance, alliteration, repetition, and wide-ranging metaphors, Nahum arrests its readers with the vivid immediacy of battle and invites them into a carefully crafted world.

Reading Nahum as literature is also a challenge, because the most common way of bearing the 'burden' of the book's violence and sexually charged rhetoric is to historicize it; the severity of Assyrian oppression becomes the explanation/justification of the vehemence of Nahum's response. Historically located readings treat Nahum as a tractate about the past, its fate enmeshed with that of Nineveh, long ago destroyed. Deprioritizing the historical dimensions of the book, as a literary reading does, forces an encounter with its harshness, one that is not softened by constantly remembering how mean the Assyrians were.

I take up the challenge that a literary reading of Nahum poses for several reasons. Primarily, a literary approach touches my own sympathies. I have grown wary of our ability to reconstruct the compositional history or the political history of biblical documents; I am not sure that there was a 'historical Nahum' whose life and times I can reconstruct. In this regard, I find attractive the position of the late Robert Carroll (1983) that behind prophetic books stand 'poets, not prophets'; these texts are intentionally constructed works of literature far more than they are edited collections of oral sermons delivered by ecstatic preachers.

Most importantly, however, reading Nahum as literature foregrounds questions that are closest to my own passions: questions of ethics. As a mother, as a woman, as one concerned about violence, I want to explore what reading this book does to the imagination and perhaps ultimately to the soul. How does this book, explicitly and implicitly, configure the ethical landscape? How do its rhetoric and symbolic world encourage its readers to think and behave?

These interests, and others that will become clearer in the course of my discussion, lead me to employ various types of literary approaches— including formalist literary criticism, intertextuality, ideological critique, and deconstruction. My assumption throughout is that an appreciation of the artistry of this book facilitates an understanding of the powerful effects it has on its readers and allows us to enter into more fruitful dialogue with Nahum's ethical world.

I. Reading Nahum Historically

Apart from a few explicitly literary treatments of Nahum,[1] the book has been treated primarily in historical terms. In the pages that follow, I attempt to explain and then evaluate 'historical' readings of Nahum.

A. Nahum Historicized

1. *Finding a date*. While a minority of voices has maintained that Nahum dates to the exilic or postexilic periods,[2] much more common is its location in the seventh century BCE, when Assyria remained a formidable and very real threat to Judah. Such confidence stems from the application of a traditional dictum of biblical studies: a piece of literature can have been written neither *before* the events it describes as passed nor *after* the events it describes as in the future. Using this logic, Nahum must have been composed after the fall of Thebes (assumed by 3.8-10) and before the fall of Nineveh (for which it calls), the dates of which are generally accepted as 663 and 612 BCE, respectively. Attempting to narrow the time frame for the book within this range, Van der Woude (1977) sets the book's composition between 660 and 630 by exiles of the Northern kingdom who fled south after the Assyrian destruction. Christensen (1999: 200), who connects Nahum with Manasseh's revolt in 2 Chronicles 33, sets Nahum in 652–648 BCE. Cathcart (1992) points to 625 BCE, when Nabopolassar's ascendency would have encouraged those who were opposed to the Assyrians.

Secondary arguments for dating Nahum point to the literature with which Nahum can be shown to be in direct relation. The book, for example, cannot have been composed after the late Hasmonean period, since it is cited in great detail in *Pesher Nahum* from Qumran. Similarly, Nahum cannot postdate Josephus, who cites Nahum in his *Antiquities* (9.11.3).[3]

Theoretically, the earliest date for the book could be set by dating the literature that Nahum itself quotes. But, as I will demonstrate below in a study of redaction criticism, many scholars are unwilling to date an entire book according to its latest material. For example, Nogalski,

---

1.   Marks 1987; Patterson and Travers 1990; an extensive listing of literary devices is given in Wendland 1998: 165.

2.   Mason (1991: 75) outlines those who date in the postexilic period.

3.   Nogalski does argue that Habakkuk and Jonah draw from Nahum, but in such small snippets that defending the existence of an actual book of Nahum by the time of these books is difficult (Nogalski 1993a, 1993b). The history of the book's interpretation is treated in Christensen (1999) and in Ball (1999).

whose two monographs argue painstakingly for directions of influence in and on the Book of the Twelve, maintains that parts of Nahum must be postexilic since it quotes from Deutero-Isaiah and Isaiah 1–39.[4] He nonetheless posits that the corpus 'had a structured literary form prior to the post-exilic reshaping... The early corpus had a frame predicting the death of the king in spite of the Assyrians' numerical strength' (Nogalski 1993b: 123-24). Nogalski (1993b: 128) dates this early layer of Nahum to 612 BCE: 'Of utmost significance for dating the earlier portions of Nahum around the time of Nineveh's destruction is the basic tenor of the passages which treat the city Nineveh as a political entity, not as symbol for all nations.' Clearly, the dating of Nahum to the Assyrian period is well entrenched.

2. *What to do with a date.* Dating Nahum's composition to the height of the Assyrian period is enticing to scholars for several reasons. First, such a connection gives the biblical interpreter a significant supplemental corpus on which to draw.

Historians have been fascinated with Assyrian materials since at least the nineteenth century, when early attempts at ancient Near Eastern archaeology began at Nineveh, Calah, and Dur-Sharrukin. The first-person accounts of the pioneers who excavated these Assyrian cities exuded their conviction that the material remains in their hands were not only awe-inspiring but also crucial to understanding the past. As Hilprecht's early twentieth-century account indicates, these explorers believed that they had solved the puzzle of ancient history (1903: 118-19):

> Without the knowledge of a single cuneiform character, we learned the principal events of Sennacherib's government, and from a mere study of those sculptured walls we got familiar with the customs and habits of the ancient Assyrians, at the same time obtaining a first clear glance of the whole civilization of western Asia.

In the 1850s, advances in the decipherment of cuneiform offered the keys to these treasures. The extensive documentary remains unearthed by Layard at the royal library of Nineveh and at Sennacherib's palace intrigued not only Assyriologists but also biblical scholars. Suddenly, a world previously known only through the Bible and classical sources was

---

4.   Nah. 1.9-11 draws from Isa. 10 and Nah. 1.12-14 from Isa. 52 (Nogalski 1993b: 113, 115, 128). Although Nah. 1.2 obviously alludes to Exod. 34.6-7, the creed is so well distributed among the biblical material as to be considered traditional and formulaic.

illumined by texts, art, and architecture, and the veracity of the Bible seemed assured. Hilprecht's enthusiasm ran rampant (1903: 119):

> How much the interpretation of the Old Testament books profited from Layard's epoch-making discoveries, we can scarcely realize… It was not only through analogy and comparison that so many obscure words and passages in the Scripture received fresh light and often an entirely new meaning—sometimes the very same persons and events mentioned in the historical and prophetical books of the Bible were depicted on those monuments or recorded in their accompanying descriptions.

Holloway traces how the Assyrian finds resonated with two themes in British culture of the period—nationalism and the desire for biblical proof. Locked in competition with France both over Ottoman territory and over 'the proprietorship of the past' (Holloway 2000), Britain's prestige was bolstered by its ability to uncover ancient treasures and to display them on home soil—a prestige which the archaeologist G. Rawlinson saw as mandatory for British control of subject masses (Holloway 2000: 11). (The frontispiece to Layard's reports from Assyria shows the striking distinction between the British archaeologists and their 'native' subjects; see Plate 1.) The confirmation of the biblical record also bolstered a strongly Christian nation that was beleaguered by social change and the challenges posed by natural science and (German) Higher Criticism of the Bible (Holloway 2000: 3). Indeed, as Searight demonstrates, the connections that were drawn between Assyrian documents and the Bible generated not only interest in but also financial support for continued excavations (1979: 213).

Holloway traces, too, how rapidly the images of Assyrian finds became part of the aesthetic culture of Britain and the West. Engravings of the lion-headed bulls that once flanked Assyrian palaces, along with images of native bedouin, were extravagantly printed and widely produced, soon taking their place as 'biblical' illustrations, both in scholarly and popular publications. The discovery of Assyrian texts and artifacts gave those interested in the Bible both external confirmation of its validity and material goods to buy and sell.

While Assyriology in the twenty-first century has changed a great deal since its nineteenth-century origins, it retains its strong allure for biblical scholars. Over a hundred years of analysis and publication have made the texts and images of Assyria widely accessible for study and illustration. Expanding the fairly limited historical and linguistic scope of the Hebrew Bible, Assyrian materials offer additional insights into the religious and social matrix of the ancient Near East; provide a cognate language with which obscure Hebrew words can be compared; and offer extensive royal archives that aid in the reconstruction of biblical chronology. And, unlike biblical manuscripts, they come with pictures—pictures that can be studied and reproduced for the marketing of biblical textbooks, handbooks, dictionaries, and commentaries.

Second, Assyrian material finds are appealing to biblical scholars also because they aid in corroborating the biblical value judgment on the Assyrians, agreeing with the Bible that the Assyrians were formidable, brutal warriors. Assyrian royal inscriptions attest not only the army's facility with iron weapons and siege technology but also its systematic brutal treatment of captives: the slaughter of tens of thousands, the deportation of large population groups (some to slave labor camps), and the selective blinding, flaying, and impalement of enemies—both alive and dead. Ashurnasirpal boasts (Roux 1980: 269-70):

> I built a pillar over against his city gate and I flayed all the chiefs who had revolted, and I covered the pillar with their skin. Some I walled up within the pillar, some I impaled upon the pillar on stakes, and others I bound to stakes round the pillar...and the limbs of the officers, of the royal officers who had rebelled... Many of the captives from among them I burned with fire, and many I took as living captives. From some I cut off their noses, their ears and their fingers, of many I put out the eyes. I made one pillar of the living and another of heads, and I bound their heads to tree trunks round about the city. Their young men and maidens I burned in fire. Twenty men I captured alive and I immured them in the wall of his palace... The rest of their warriors I consumed with thirst in the desert of the Euphrates.

The Assyrian kings advertise themselves as ruthless, a tactic which Grayson (1992: 748) describes as psychological warfare, 'calculated frightfulness'.

As Winter (1981) demonstrates, the art of the palace reliefs mirrors the testimony of the texts, likewise showing the supreme lordship of the Assyrian king and the invincible nature of his army. In myriad wall reliefs from Nimrud and Nineveh, larger-than-life Assyrian kings hunt and stand victorious over muscle-bound, snarling lions, caught in the process of excruciatingly painful deaths (see Plate 2). An even more frequent motif is the celebration of war. In crowded, stylized scenes, repeated over and over throughout the palace reliefs, Assyrian soldiers trample vanquished enemies underfoot and carry baskets of enemy heads; bodies hang limp, impaled on stakes; women, bareheaded, are carted away with other booty (see Plates 3-5).

Bersani and Dutoit (1985: 3), comparing Assyrian self-glorification with Leni Riefenstahl's pro-Hitler film *Triumph of the Will*, explain the effect of such scenes on the viewer:

> The celebratory nature of the reliefs, the obvious relish with which the
> defeat, humiliation, and slaughter of Assyria's enemies are portrayed, and
> the profusely gory detail of the battle and the hunting scenes, would seem
> to confirm the historians' view of the Assyrians as an intensely nationalistic,
> imperialistic, and violent people.

The stark, consistent portrait of Assyria as a bloodthirsty, ruthless culture
serves for many readers as an important interpretive lens through which
the Bible's harsh proclamations against Assyria are to be viewed. Any call
for or rejoicing over the demise of such a brutal nation is seen not just
as understandable but, indeed, as righteous; Assyria becomes the
oppressor against whom a literature of resistance is morally justified,
even demanded.

   For these reasons, the connections between Assyrian history and the
book of Nahum become important for many commentators. Roberts
(1991), for example, explains the leonine imagery in Nah. 2.12 by
appealing to Assyrian iconography. Even more consistently, commentators explain that Assyrian cruelty accounts for Nahum's harsh, graphic
call for violence against Nineveh and its inhabitants:

> God's vengeance upon Nineveh puts an end to Judah's oppression and
> humiliation and implies the breaking of Judah's yoke and bonds... There
> is, then, not a trace of tension or inconsistency between God's goodness
> and God's retributive wrath (Peels 1995: 205).

> The text of Nahum gives expression to strong emotions of anger and
> frustration due to real life experience of lack of freedom and oppression...
> Does the rage against Assyria have any warrant? Is there ground for such
> rage? For a great part of the monarchical history of Israel and Judah,
> Assyria played a major role... Assyria ruled with brutal force and power...
> Oppressive societies are the birthplace of mainsprings of remarkable and
> powerful poetry that voices the dissatisfaction of those or on the behalf of
> those experiencing lack of freedom and misery... It is easy to see how a
> Judean consciousness, formed by well over one hundred years of Assyrian
> hegemony and buttressed by brutal militarism and propaganda, could
> react with elation at the news of Assyria's collapse (García-Treto 1996:
> 595).

   Although I will explore extensively in 'Nahum and Atrocity' the way in
which commentators have attempted to explain and contain the violence
of Nahum, here I have suggested the significant role that setting Nahum
within the Assyrian period plays in many treatments of the ethics of the
book. When it is read within the Assyrian period, Nahum becomes the
cry of the oppressed.

B. Problems with 'History'

While clearly enticing to scholars and liberation theologians, reading Nahum in an Assyrian context is not without problems. As I explain below, I wish neither to advance a philosophical argument against 'history' nor to deny the experience of the oppressed. But here I do aim to call attention to the instability of common historical readings of Nahum.

1. *The problem of editing.* The prophetic books are widely recognized to have undergone extensive editing. Indeed, redaction criticism, the scholarly method for distinguishing later additions from the work of the original author, continues to be a primary method by which prophetic books are studied.

For most of its history, redaction criticism granted a privileged status to the 'original' layers of prophetic books, considering the redactional layers as intrusions. Confident in the technology of their trade, early redaction critics touted their method as a refining fire that could burn off the dross of the editor and leave behind the pure utterance of the man of God. In 1947, for example, Raymond Calkins (1947: 7) assured a lay public that redaction criticism is a boon to the faithful reader:

> A vast amount of the most painstaking scholarship in recent years has been devoted to the work of restoring these prophecies to their original form by removing these successive layers of later deposits of material, and deleting the inapt (*sic*) scribal insertions which have crept into the text. To this scholarship the Bible student is deeply indebted. Instead of viewing it as laying a rough hand on sacred and inviolable books, one should rather regard it as a reverent effort to give us of this day the authentic messages of these inspired men just as they fell from their lips.

Current trends in prophetic scholarship have challenged redaction criticism's confidence that it can isolate the kernel of the book, and especially the assumption that the 'original' kernel preserves the oral speeches of a historical, individual prophet. Robert Carroll, perhaps most vocal in this discussion, insisted that in prophetic books we have the work not of prophets but of poets, 'intellectuals' (1983: 25). According to Carroll, prophets such as Jeremiah are fictional characters created for the purposes of the books that bear their names, and the historical introductions to the prophetic books were crafted by an author in order to invent the ancient prophets as biographical figures (1988: 25).

Increasingly in prophetic studies, even those who remain open to the historical reality of prophets refuse to prioritize the 'original' layer the book. Instead, they argue that editors, not prophets, should be considered the authors of prophetic books. While editors may have used some traditional materials, it was they who created books about prophets—addressing the needs of their own communities by crafting books for the sake of readers, not of historical accuracy (see e.g. Ben Zvi 1991).

The shift from treating editorial additions as subtractable additions to perceiving them as integral to the book can be seen nowhere so clearly as in the case of prophetic superscriptions. Scholars have long agreed that superscriptions were not penned by the prophets themselves but by an editor, in order to provide context to the prophetic oracles and continuity between books. Because prophetic superscriptions agree with the royal chronology outlined in Samuel through Kings (known as the Deuteronomistic History), they are usually credited to an exilic Deuteronomistic editor. Some scholars date the superscriptions even later, to the Persian period, when anxieties about annihilation induced by the exile and Persian imperial encouragement to record ancestral laws converged to instigate the production of a national literature. Until recently, the recognition that superscriptions were written after the fact did not prevent scholars from utilizing the information that they provide in a fairly positivistic way. Prophetic books have continued to be dated according to the kings mentioned in their opening verses, based on the assumptions that the superscriptions, while late, are reliable and that a book's date is that of the prophet's career rather than of the book's formation.

When, as in the new trends I have described, the latter assumption is challenged and the question given priority is 'When was this book put together in this form?', superscriptions take on a different significance. They no longer offer a contemporary snapshot of a prophet, or even the reminiscences of a group of 'disciples' (Tucker 1977: 67; Carroll 1988: 28), but instead serve as one clue as to how a community remembered or created figures from the past. From the standpoint of their final form, the superscriptions dictate the temporal setting in which the material is to be understood. E. Ben Zvi makes a strong case for such an understanding of Zephaniah's superscription:

> The community was asked to read a written text about a prophet, or more precisely, about a specific 'word of God' that was given in the past to a certain character in the book.[5]

---

5. Ben Zvi 1996: 129. So, too, Collins (1993: 31): 'The historical value of the prophetical books lies, therefore, in the insight which they give us into exilic and postexilic thought, rather than as a guide to the history of prophecy in Israel.'

> The author does not claim to be a prophet. He or she wrote a book about
> the word of YHWH that came to a prophet in the past, and writing a book
> about the prophecies putatively delivered by a prophet at a certain time in
> the past is clearly a different activity than prophesying (Ben Zvi 1991: 349).

2. *A historical Nahum?* Most scholars discern in Nahum signs of heavy
redactional activity. The book's translational difficulties, especially the
frequency with which pronouns lack antecedents, are often credited to
less-than-judicious editing. The distinctive style and tone of the opening
portrait of Yahweh in 1.2-10 is also taken as evidence that a once-
independent hymn or liturgy was incorporated into an otherwise narrow
book, shifting an exclusive attention to the downfall of Nineveh to a
larger vision of God's awesome power. Nogalski attributes these and
other redactions of Nahum to the process of its inclusion into an inte-
grated Book of the Twelve.

Given the usual ways in which Nahum is studied, the contemporary
shift to treating redaction as authorship has significant implications for
understanding this book. Opaque vocabulary, ambiguous pronouns, and
shifts in style become deliberate authorial strategies rather than marks of
carelessness. Dating, too, is challenged: if the book bears exilic or
postexilic elements, as Nogalski claims, then a truly historical reading of
Nahum would consider the book's function in a postexilic, rather than in
a pre-exilic, setting.

The shift to seeing superscriptions as redactors' creation of literary
settings for their pieces clearly affects an understanding of Nahum. Our
ability to connect the book with a prophet, especially one named
Nahum, depends solely upon 1.1; only here do we learn the prophet's
name and discern the genre markers that distinguish a prophetic book.
The book itself contains no prophetic call narrative, no account of
prophetic actions—indeed, no narrative of any kind. If Nahum's superscription is indeed a redactor's attempt to invoke the memory or the
fiction of a prophet, then the personality of the true author remains
hidden.

Similarly, a literary understanding of Nahum's superscription dis-
lodges the book's historical anchor. The conclusion that the book must
predate 612 BCE because it speaks of Nineveh as a city not yet fallen
relies on the assumption that it was authored by the Nahum described in
the superscription. If the entire book is the work of a redactor, then its
purpose becomes no longer the prediction of Nineveh's doom by a
prophet of the Assyrian period but rather the attempt of a redactor/
author to instruct his own community by asking them to consider what
an earlier prophet had said about the demise of a well-remembered foe.

(Both the success of Assyrian propaganda and the witness of biblical materials would have assured that the memory of Assyrian brutality long outlasted the kingdom itself.)

While historical memory may lie behind the book of Nahum, the book itself is a literary presentation of that history, one that calls for sustained attention to its literary style. As Hutcheon explains (1989: 58; 81):

> We only have access to the past today through its traces—its documents, the testimony of witnesses, and of other archival materials. In other words, we only have representations of the past from which to construct our narrative explanations.

> To say that the past is only *known* to us through textual traces is not, however, the same as saying that the past is only textual...past events existed empirically, but in epistemological terms we can only know them today through texts.

Highlighting the textual, literary nature of Nahum does not contest the 'reality' of the seventh century BCE; but it does underscore that, even if a historical Nahum did speak within the period of the 'real' Assyrians, our knowledge of both is mediated to us by documents—pieces of literature that bring with them the ambiguities of interpretation that mark all literature.[6] My claim is that the historical Assyria is much less important for understanding the book of Nahum than what the book itself wants us to know—the rhetorical Assyria that Nahum creates. My understanding of Nahum will rest less on Assyriology than on questions such as, 'What does the rhetoric of this book lead me to believe about Assyria?' and 'How is that construct of Nineveh necessary to my assent to the book's vision of what should happen to it?'

II. Alternative Angles of Vision

The questions that I have posed can be explored only by careful study of the language of the book of Nahum. Here I explain the methods and perspectives that will guide that literary project.

A. Rhetorical Dimensions

My primary question in this commentary is how the piece of literature we call Nahum creates in the mind of its reader a mental map of the world. I want to know how Nahum's rhetoric invites readers to envision

---

6.   As I will explore further in the chapter on 'Nahum and Atrocity', the Assyrian royal inscriptions and palace reliefs themselves require interpretation. Bersani and Dutoit (1985: 9) demonstrate how stylistic features in Assyrian art draw the viewer's attention to the playfulness of the images, away from mimetic representation.

Assyria, Judah, Yahweh, and other characters, and how those images shape a reader's thoughts and, perhaps, behaviors. I am interested not only in *what* Nahum does to a reader but also *how* it does it. What are the tricks of Nahum's rhetorical trade?

I realize that in talking about the agency of a text, the ability of a piece of literature to shape the production of meaning, I enter (and take sides in) a long-standing and contentious debate about where 'meaning' resides: in the text itself? in readers? in the interpretive communities that have shaped a reader?

While these debates are important, Stout helpfully underscores that they are exacerbated by our use of vocabulary (cited in Fowl 1998: 56-65). Masked by the simplicity of the word 'meaning' is the practical reality that our efforts in reading do not necessarily have the same goals in mind. Fowl, agreeing with Stout, calls for a greater precision in terms: we should abandon talk about 'meaning' in favor of other terms that will both suit our interpretive interests and be precise enough to put a stop to futile discussions (Fowl 1998: 57-58).

In response to Fowl's call for precision, I name my own project as exploring the questions:

- How do the word choices, images, metaphors, and style of the book of Nahum configure Nineveh, Judah, Yahweh, and enemies?
- What is privileged and not privileged by the book's literary style?
- What modes of thinking and action does that presentation encourage in a reader?
- How does a sequential reading of Nahum shape the reading process?

The description of my task is further complicated when I refer to '*the* reader'. Again, fervent discussions in literary study highlight the diversity of readers, how the fiction of a generic reader attempts to obscure the reality of real-life readers, who from discrete social locations read quite differently. I do not deny the validity of this debate, nor do I think it has an easy solution. Attempts to sidestep the question by configuring the reader as a heuristic construct (an imagined reader, implied reader, etc.) are unhelpful in my judgment because they remain text-centered approaches and because they fail to take into account historical, diverse readers.

On one level, then, 'the reader' about whom I am talking is myself. I am considering what Nahum's rhetoric is doing to *me* and to the readers that I choose to consult and cite. I am asking how the formal literary features, the structure, and the intertexts of this book lead me to think, to imagine, to construct. Such a starting point recognizes that my conclusions about what happens to the reader of Nahum cannot be defended by an epistemological argument but only by persuasion. My intention is to describe the process of reading Nahum in a way that is helpful and persuasive to other readers as they seek to make sense of this book, especially its most troubling parts. To that end, I put my own readings of Nahum into dialogue with those of other readers—both those discussed in the final chapters and those who read this commentary.

B. Ideological Dimensions

This rhetorical task is intimately related to ideological criticism, which seeks to name the assumptions that undergird the rhetorical worlds that texts present, particularly the distribution of power they presuppose. In the description provided by *PmB*: 274-75:

> Ideological criticism has as its primary purpose the task of exposing and charting the structure and dynamics of these power relations as they come to expression in language, in conflicting ideologies operating in discourse, and in flesh and blood readers of texts in their concrete social locations and relationships... Texts are implicated in both the representation and reproduction of ideology.

As a critical approach, ideological criticism is concerned with the different ways in which power relations are manifested, and it has a particular interest in issues of race, class, and gender. My feminist interests will be evident throughout the commentary but especially in my discussion of the personification of Nineveh as a woman in Nahum 3 and in 'Nahum and (Wo)men'. Issues of race and class are broached in my discussion of how the book of Nahum configures the Other, particularly in 'Nahum and Atrocity'.

Stephen Fowl has argued that an enterprise like the one I have described is misleading, since 'Texts Don't Have Ideologies' (1995). According to Fowl, the fact that a given text can be pressed into the service of multiple, competing ideologies indicates that ideologies are, instead, in readers and in their communities. While Fowl is right to point out that specific applications of texts to ideological aims are fluid, I believe his argument fails to take into account the features of a text that place it at the center of ideological debate. For example, in his demonstration that readers have used the story of Abraham quite differently, Fowl indeed shows that readers diverge in their conclusions about what a text 'means'. But he does not recognize that the readers he cites agree that the underlying question of the Abraham narrative is that of who is included (and excluded): on that level of deep, underlying ideologies (e.g. of 'us' vs 'them'), those 'differing' readers in fact agree. I concur with Fowl that texts are not fixed objects independent of their reading and that a reader brings to reading pre-existing ideologies. I argue, however, that the ability of a reader to engage with a text at all requires that the text and the reader share certain assumptions and, if not ideologies themselves, then at least the ability to recognize the categories in which ideologies are framed.

C. Other Literary Methods

1. *Formalist literary criticism.* Any attention to the book's represent-ation of reality requires sustained attention to the artfulness of its lan-guage, the formal literary features that give it texture and shape. Nahum is well known for its high level of literary artistry. Most strikingly in Nahum 2–3, where the downfall of Nineveh is portrayed, vivid imagery, alliteration, onomatopoeia, and stark metaphorical comparisons arrest the reader. A writer in the first half of the twentieth century raved (Macarthur, quoted in Preminger and Greenstein 1986: 505):

> The superb strong word-pictures and the astoundingly impetuous move-ment place the author among the world's great literary artists. We still can see the flaming chariots with their scarlet-clad warriors; we still can hear the noise of the whip and the noise of the rattling of the wheels, and of the prancing horses, and of the jumping chariots. Brilliant pictures, replete with vivid realism, follow in quick succession—the preparation, the repul-ses, the flight, the spoils, the heaps of corpses… We read the book for sheer artistic enjoyment. Nothing can deprive Nahum of his place as one of the strongest, most spirited, and vivid of poets.

In addition to demonstrating a high level of literary craft, the language of Nahum is also extremely complex. As I have noted above, its vocabulary is uncommon, and pronouns shift repeatedly in number and gender with rare indication of their antecedents. Often, the problem is diagnosed either as a product of sloppy redaction or as the result of errors in scribal copying. In turn, the text is 'cured' by emendation. J.J.M. Roberts's (1991) commentary, for example, proposes large numbers of changes to the text, and Cathcart's (1973) volume is devoted to the possibility that northwest Semitic philology might help decipher some of Nahum's textual enigmas. As I will point out along the way, standard English translations often emend the text of Nahum to produce more coherent readings.

My own response to the strangeness of Nahum's language is to read the Masoretic Text (MT) as it stands from a literary perspective, while acknowledging the solutions of modern English translations and biblical scholars. I do not read with the MT out of an illusion that it is a pristine or 'original' text, or even with the understanding that it is *the* final form of the text. The MT does, however, witness to *an* extant text. Unlike reconstructed, eclectic texts, it may be understood to have stood as a literary whole at some stage of its history. Out of curiosity, I am interested in how the difficult language within that literary whole might function: how can a text's ambiguities and puzzles be seen to function in their larger context? What do shifts in pronouns and tenses do to the reading process?

2. *Intertextuality*. The rhetorical force of Nahum derives not only from the book itself but also from its resonances with other literature. While the term 'intertextuality' is sometimes used to describe the tracing of historical relationships between documents (which one came first and what the direction of dependence was), my own use of 'intertextuality' follows the work of Julia Kristeva and Mikhail Bakhtin, who consider interrelationships between materials on the level of text reception, looking for the synchronic collision and collusion of texts.[7]

On one level, such a use of intertextuality blends with genre theory. That is, similarities between texts (in style, vocabulary, organization, etc.) invite readers to draw connections between them. Tolbert, following Kermode, focuses on an author's intentional use of genre markers and defines genre as 'a prior agreement between authors and readers or as a set of shared expectations or as a consensus of fore-understandings exterior to a text which enable us to follow that text' (Tolbert 1989: 49; cf. Kermode 1979: 163). Reading intertextually along the lines of Kristeva, however, does not rely upon the determination of authorial intention: assumptions of what constitutes a genre can be—and are—made by readers regardless of the author's own choice of models.

On another level, Kristevan intertextuality has a destabilizing effect. Reading multiple texts synchronically produces new readings of each, and their juxtaposition often uncovers what a text has left unsaid, concealed, and complicates efforts to discern the meaning of a given text. According to Beal (1992a: 23):

> The basic force of intertextuality is to problematize, even spoil, textual boundaries—those lines of demarcation which allow a reader to talk about *the* meaning, subject, or origin of a writing. Such borders, intertextuality asserts, are never solid or stable. Texts are always spilling over into other texts.

In reading Nahum, I look for the ways in which reading it alongside its intertexts (other prophetic literature, other texts that begin with the

7. For an application of Kristeva and Bakhtin to biblical narratives, see Beal 1992b.

term *maśśā'*, other biblical descriptions of Assyria, etc.) illumines both what Nahum says and what it obscures.

3. *Deconstruction*. Deconstructive readings produce many of the same destabilizing results as Kristevan intertextuality. Like intertextuality, deconstruction seeks out what a text does not say, or rather how it occasionally 'slips' to speak what it had intended to hide. As a method, however, deconstruction operates on a more linguistic basis than does intertextuality. Deconstruction starts with structuralism's observation that language functions by distinguishing opposites: light is known by being not dark; big is the opposite of little. Ideologically speaking, texts (if not language itself) privilege one member of the pair: light is better than dark; we are better than they. As a method, deconstruction scrutinizes texts for the points at which oppositional language and/or valuations fissure—the slip of the pen or of the psyche where dark is better than light, where we and they are the same.

In reading Nahum, which relies heavily on the contrast of opposites (Judah vs Assyria, 'you' vs 'us', male vs female), I watch for consistency and notice where Nahum 'slips' in its alignments and allegiances. As I explore most thoroughly in the final chapters, a recognition of these slips serves in the formulation of one response to Nahum's explicit misogyny and violence.

D. Why Does it Matter?

My real interest in rhetorical and ideological readings lies in their ability to create a space for the discussion of ethics within the critical enterprise.

> The ethical question, therefore, belongs at the heart of the ideological discussion... Ideological criticism, we might conclude, at root has to do with the ethical character of and response to the text and to those lived relations that are represented and reproduced in the act of reading (*PmB*: 275).

I am interested in ethics, both descriptively and normatively. By 'descriptive ethics' I refer to a consideration of how a text configures 'the good', how through various techniques a piece of literature develops a vision of what—and who—matters. In this enterprise, I draw on the work of Martha Nussbaum, who claims (1990: 5):

> A view of life is told. The telling itself—the selection of genre, formal structures, sentences, vocabulary, of the whole manner of addressing the reader's sense of life—all of this expresses a sense of life and of value, a sense of what matters and what does not, of what learning and communicating are, of life's relations and connection.

As I read Nahum, I am asking about its 'sense of life', how it sees and values the world. I look not only at its explicit value judgments—for example, calling Yahweh 'good' in 1.7 and Nineveh a 'whore' in 3.4—but also the implicit value judgments of its descriptions of war and varying levels of personalization of characters. I look, too, at what—and whom—Nahum leaves unnamed.

Yet I am uninterested in remaining a detached observer of Nahum's sensibilities. Nahum raises issues that touch on my own 'sense of life', issues that matter deeply to me. I want to engage Nahum in a normative discussion of ethics.

> Ideological criticism demands a high level of self-consciousness and makes an explicit, unabashed appeal to justice. As an ethically grounded act, ideological reading tends to raise critical consciousness about what is just and unjust about those lived relations that Althusser describes, and to change those power relationships for the better. It challenges readers to accept political responsibility for themselves and for the world in which they live (*PmB*: 275).

In a vastly multicultural world, I know that I cannot appeal to universally-held values or assume that all readers will critique and value Nahum for the same things I do. Rather than argue for a theory of ethics, instead I attempt to name the commitments and convictions that drive my reading.

The book of Nahum both attracts and repels me ethically. On the one hand, I find much of it disturbing. The violence of the book feels all too familiar in a world of the Holocaust and Palestinian refugee camps; of Armenian, Cambodian, Rwandan, and Albanian genocides; of skinheads; of students who gun down their classmates and their teachers—a world that I want to change. I tend toward pacifism, and Nahum celebrates war.

Even more disturbing to me is the relish with which the destruction of enemies is described, the joy that it takes in envisioning, in painstaking detail, the humiliation and death of others. Nahum tries to keep the enemies generic, so that I need never look into their eyes. But my own commitments conjure the faces of Nahum's enemies. As a woman, I see myself and women like me as the Nineveh who is stripped and raped, and I am horrified that someone would gloat over 'our' degradation. As a mother, I want Nahum to express regret that the innocent suffer for the crimes of the guilty, and I cringe when, in an offhand remark, it mentions the death of children (Nah. 3.10).

On the other hand, my commitment to allow the perspective of the oppressed to challenge that of my own privilege pulls me to Nahum, listening for what I as a white American might learn about the realities and horrors of war, how justice looks from the underside. Aware (though never sufficiently) of my own tendency toward arrogant reading, I cannot dismiss Nahum as ethically inferior or silence Nahum's voice with my own 'No'.

In my reading, Nahum has not only literary intertexts but social and ethical intertexts as well—hate crimes, acts of domestic and ethnic violence, the struggles of the oppressed, questions of justice. Reading this book draws attention to some of my most fundamental ethical questions, questions which I seek—in reading as well as in living—to wrestle for whatever blessing they might leave behind.

Nahum 1.1. The Burden of Nineveh: The Book of the Vision of Nahum the Elkoshite

> Beginning is not only a kind of action; it is also a frame of mind, a kind of
> work, an attitude, a consciousness (Said 1985: xv).

In our project to trace the contours of the 'sense of life' that the book of
Nahum narrates, we do well to pay particular attention to the way in
which it begins. Literary beginnings, like those of movies and of relationships, are fraught with meaning. They are orienting discourse, not only
explicitly by providing labels for the kind of literature to follow and by
introducing us to casts of characters but also *implicitly* by determining
what vocabulary will be spoken and what language will be permitted.
Beginnings instruct us in how to read and what to read for. They invite
readers into specific symbolic universes and by definition de-authorize
others. In the words of Edward Said (1985: 16), 'Every sort of writing
establishes explicit and implicit rules of pertinence for itself: certain
things are admissible, certain others not'.

I. Reading Nahum as a Prophetic Book

One way of understanding the framing function of beginnings is to
recognize that they precipitate the reader's first assumptions about the
genre of the material at hand. Because 'what readers conceive the genre
of a text to be…determines how they read it, what they expect to find,
and what they learn from it' (Tolbert 1989: 48), the generic categorization of a book guides the reading process. Genre designation sets
parameters for the 'gap-filling' that readers must exercise in order to
make sense of literature—the thousands of assumptions that readers
make, often unconsciously, to connect the discrete pieces of information
a text provides into a coherent, logical whole.

Nahum's beginning is of a particular type. Sharing neither the
distinguishing features of Psalm superscriptions nor the narrative
beginnings of books like Ruth or Judges, it bears the formal clues of the
prophetic superscription. As outlined in Chart 1 (at the end of this chapter), all of the fifteen prophetic books (excluding Daniel, given its different style and placement in the Jewish canon) name a prophet; nine
list his family and/or geographical origin; and nine offer some indication
of the prophet's time period. Moreover, all fifteen prophetic super-

scriptions mark the composition that follows with one or more of three labels: 'word' or 'words' (*dābar* or *dᵉbārîm*); 'vision' (*ḥᵃzôn*); and/or 'oracle/burden' (*maśśā'*).

Labeled as a *maśśā'* directed at a specific target, as a vision, and as originating from an individual from a specific place, the book of Nahum announces itself as a prophetic book. Nahum's beginning serves as a genre marker indicating that the book is to be read as other prophetic books are read, opening them as intertexts.

A. Reading Nahum with the Latter Prophets

While the individual books of the Latter Prophets likely went through complex and diverse stages of composition, in their final redacted form the books bear much in common: 'Despite their different histories they have all ended up looking broadly similar as books from the point of view of their contents, themes, imagery and general shape' (Collins 1993: 19). Not all features appear in all prophetic books, but some features are frequent enough to suggest that a reader of a 'prophetic' book might bring to the task the following expectations.

1. *Expected contents.* The two most common types of material in prophetic books are: (1) oracles of salvation; and (2) oracles of judgment, here understood not as formal genres but as descriptions of content. The latter can be further subdivided into (a) oracles of judgment against other nations; and (b) oracles of judgment against Israel and/or Judah. Several observations about the common permutations of these oracles within the prophetic material prove instructive.

First, in the final forms of the books, oracles of judgment against Israel and/or Judah never stand without accompanying oracles of salvation, or at least some intimation of good fortune. In the cases of Amos and Hosea, salvific promises close books that are otherwise focused on judgment. In the case of Isaiah, judgment and salvation are interwoven throughout the book.

Second, the prophetic material regarding other nations appears predominately in the context of judgment. While foreign nations sometimes are delegated tasks within the divine plan, no oracles of salvation for other nations correspond with those for Israel and/or Judah. A frequent feature of prophetic books are the extended Oracles against the Nations (OAN), to be discussed below.

Third, the judgment against other nations is always related to salvation for Israel and/or Judah. The two are often connected structurally—such as in Isaiah, where OAN in 13–23 are followed by images of salvation for Judah in 25–26; and in Ezekiel, where words against the nations in

25–32 give way to Judah's consolation in 37. A more explicit relationship between 'their' judgment and 'our' salvation is drawn in Obadiah, where punishment against Edom is offered as remedy for its treatment of Judah.

2. *Expected political dimensions.* The superscriptions, and occasionally also the contents, of the Latter Prophets place a given prophet's activity within the context of a major national event in Israel/Judah's history: the fall of Samaria (Amos, Hosea, Isaiah, Micah), the fall of Judah (Jeremiah, Ezekiel), or the rebuilding of the Second Temple (Haggai, Zechariah). While the connection between the prophetic word and ancient geo-politics may reflect actual historical conditions, their literary effect is significant: readers expect prophets to address real, important events, and they read to discern the prophet's historical setting, even when the book itself bears few clues.

3. *Expected temporal dimensions.* In prophetic books, prophets often speak of events prior to their actualization. For example, while the prophetic words attributed to Haggai and Zechariah seem to address a contemporaneous building project, the words of Amos and Jeremiah are presented as delivered prior to the fall of their respective nations, and the final form of Isaiah includes a mention of Cyrus the Persian, who lived two hundred years after the date given for Isaiah in the book's superscription. Reading a book as prophetic, then, raises not only the expectation that it will address a concrete historical event but also, as implied in the superscription, the possibility that the prophet will speak of events to take place beyond his own lifetime

4. *Expected authority.* Various literary features of the books of the Latter Prophets invite the reader to grant the material they contain divine authority. As noted in Chart 1, prophetic superscriptions label their contents as oracles (*maśśā'*) and visions (*ḥᵃzôn*), technical terms (see section II) for speech that derives from divine revelation. In books where this technical terminology is not employed, other vocabulary (such as 'he saw' in Isa. 1.1; Amos 1.1; Mic. 1.1) lends weight to the argument that the words gathered here are the result of divine inspiration.

In addition, the messenger speech formula, considered by many as the speech form most characteristic of the prophets, formally identifies the words of the prophet with divine speech; the prophet is verbally por-trayed as an ancient Near Eastern messenger who, according to von Rad 1965: 37 '...completely submerged his own ego and spoke as if he were his master himself speaking to the other'. By labeling the material of the books as the reporting of those prophetic speeches, the superscriptions invite a three-way identification between (1) the words of the book; (2) the words spoken by a prophet; and (3) divine will. As Floyd (2000: 171) notes, the literary style of the prophetic books further encourages the equation of divine will and written word: the prophetic books address a reader directly, as a prophet would have addressed a hearer.

B. Reading Nahum with the Former Prophets/Deuteronomistic History

The superscriptions of the Latter Prophets in turn link them with another corpus: the books of Joshua through Kings, known in the Jewish canon as the Former Prophets and by scholars as the Deuteronomistic History (so called because of its shared perspectives with the book of Deuteronomy). This connection is established both by the fact that the superscriptions of the Latter Prophets employ the chronological schema of the Deuteronomistic History and also by the significant role that prophetic figures and statements about prophecy play within the Deuteronomistic History.

The Deuteronomistic History's representation of prophets reinforces many of the assumptions drawn from reading the Latter Prophets. For example, prophets in the Deuteronomistic History use formulaic messenger speech and issue words of both comfort and judgment. The Deuteronomistic History dramatically underscores the divine origin of prophetic speech, detailing in striking narratives the danger that awaits prophets who do not deliver faithfully the word of Yahweh (e.g. 1 Kgs 13).

The Deuteronomistic History, however, adds particular dimensions to the biblical portrait of prophets:

1. *Prophets are predictors of the future.* While perhaps implied in the fact that prophetic books often speak of events later than the setting of their superscriptions (see above), the Deuteronomistic History makes the accuracy of prediction a defining mark of true prophecy. This dictum is explicitly stated in Deut. 18.21-22:

> You may say to yourself, 'How can we recognize a word that Yahweh has not spoken?' If a prophet speaks in the name of Yahweh but the thing does not take place or prove true, it is a word that Yahweh has not spoken. The prophet has spoken it presumptuously; do not be frightened by it.

The Deuteronomistic narrator goes to great lengths to link prophecy and fulfillment: for example, the account of the division of the kingdoms claims that events fulfill the word of Yahweh as spoken to the prophet

Ahijah (1 Kgs 12.15), and the reader of Jezebel's gruesome death is reminded that the prophet Elijah had announced this precise punishment (2 Kgs 9.30-37).

2. *Prophets are the ongoing sign of Yahweh's care.* The narrative structure of the Deuteronomistic History allows it to make a point only implied in the Latter Prophets: that prophecy is a frequent, if not constant, feature of Yahweh's interaction with humans. Throughout the people's history, as portrayed by the Deuteronomistic History, prophetic figures emerge to announce divine intention—from the ultimate prophet Moses (Deut. 34.10-12); to the prophets of the United Monarchy (Samuel, Nathan, Gad); to the prophets of the divided kingdoms (Elijah, Elisha, Ahijah); to those connected with Judah's fall (Isaiah and other unnamed prophets). As Collins (1993: 135-36) explains,

> For the writers of the Deuteronomistic school of thought, a belief in God's abiding presence among his people was matched by a belief in the constant, if intermittent, presence of prophetic intermediaries of the divine word through whom the guidance that Yahweh had begun in Moses was to be continued.

3. *Prophets support the Torah's injunctions against idolatry.* The primary theme shared by the Deuteronomistic History and the book of Deuteronomy is intolerance of idolatry. Deuteronomy not only offers the frequent injunction to 'love Yahweh alone' but also ends with curses on those who worship other deities. In turn, the Deuteronomistic History demonstrates through narrative the blessings that arise from loyalty to Yahweh and the curses brought down by idolatry.

In the Deuteronomistic History, the prophets are a primary voice articulating the evils of idolatry:

> Yet Yahweh warned Israel and Judah by every prophet and every seer, saying, 'Turn from your evil ways and keep my commandments and my statutes, in accordance with all the law that I commanded your ancestors and that I sent to you by my servants the prophets'. They would not listen but were stubborn, as their ancestors had been, who did not believe in Yahweh their God (2 Kgs 17.13-14).

The connection of the activity of the prophets with the injunctions of the Torah is less frequent in the Latter Prophets (except for the ending of Malachi: 'Remember the teaching of my servant Moses, the statutes and ordinances that I commanded him at Horeb for all Israel', 3.22), but is drawn frequently by later Jewish literature:

R. Isaac said, The Prophets drew from Sinai the inspiration of all their
future utterances… Not only to the Prophets alone does this apply, but to
all the sages that are destined to arise in after days (*Tanh.*, Yitro, §11, 123a-
124b).

At least one factor in Judaism's insistence that Torah and the Prophets
proclaimed a consistent message is the canonical shape of the material,
in which the Latter Prophets are read in light of the Former.

C. Nahum as a Prophetic Book: Some Observations

I have argued that the superscription of Nahum identifies its genre as
'prophetic', linking it intertextually with the Latter Prophets and with the
Deuteronomistic History. The distinctive features of these two corpora
spill over into a reading of Nahum, setting the stage for a particular
reception of this book and its message.

Most strikingly, prophetic intertexts instruct the reader of Nahum's
superscription to attribute the material that will follow to divine
intention. The prophet himself is to be acknowledged as a reliable
messenger, but the implied voice of the book is that of Yahweh. Nahum's
authority, then, is established in the strongest possible way.

Reading Nahum within the prophetic genre also raises expectations
that it will contain announcements of judgment and salvation and that
the particular combination of the two will fall within the established
range of permutations. Particularly if this book announces judgment, a
reader will expect it to include, even if on a small scale, salvation as well.
If that judgment is directed at a foreign nation, salvation is to be
proclaimed or at least implied for Israel and/or Judah.

Moreover, the intertextual connections of Nahum's superscription
lead the reader to approach the prophet named here as a real person
who spoke in a time that is historically locatable in the history of Israel
and/or Judah. These connections open the reader to the possibility that
the prophet may speak of events beyond his own lifetime; and, if those
events are projected into the future, they encourage a reader to suspect
that what had been predicted indeed was—or will be—fulfilled.

II. The Details of Nahum's Superscription and their Effects on a Reader

I have suggested that any piece of literature that begins with a prophetic
superscription engenders numerous reading expectations. The specific
vocabulary of Nahum's superscription guides the reading process in
additional ways.

A. *maśśā'*

The difference in English translations between 'oracle' (RSV, NRSV) and 'burden' (ASV, KJV) reflects scholarly debate about the precise meaning of the Hebrew word *maśśā'*. A noun form of the verbal root *nś'*, to 'lift up', *maśśā'* is variously understood: (1) to assume 'the voice' as its object, thus signifying a technical term for prophecy (best rendered as 'oracle'); or (2) to refer to anything that is lifted up ('burden'). Vigorous discussion about the 'proper' meaning of the term can be found throughout the commentaries, but Jer. 23.33-40 suggests that ancient hearers were aware of the connections between the two terms; thus, even if *maśśā'* were a technical term for a prophetic utterance, its aural association with 'heaviness, burden' would have been common for an ancient hearer/reader.

Nahum's designation as a *maśśā'* has the additional effect of connecting it with a network of other texts. The same term introduces collections that begin at Hab. 1.1; Zech. 9.1; 12.1; Mal. 1.1, and, more importantly, the extended diatribes against foreign nations in Isaiah 13–23. The Isaiah texts fit the additional category of OAN, extended prophetic speeches announcing Yahweh's intentions toward nations other than Israel and Judah.

1. *Habakkuk, Zechariah 9, Zechariah 12, and Malachi*. In each of these prophetic collections, Yahweh appears in bold theophany to act decisively on Judah's behalf. In Habakkuk 3 and Zechariah 9, Yahweh bursts in as a Divine Warrior, before whom mountains and enemies tremble, intent on saving the faithful (Hab. 3.16b; Zech. 9.16). Malachi 3 announces Yahweh's sudden appearance in the Temple to refine the priesthood.

Both Habakkuk and Malachi explicitly portray the theophany as Yahweh's response to those who question divine justice. Yahweh's appearance silences Habakkuk's complaint that 'the law becomes slack and justice never prevails… [Why is Yahweh] silent when the wicked swallow those more righteous than they?' (Hab. 1.4, 13); and in Malachi the people's question, 'Where is the God of justice?' (Mal. 2.17), is answered by the promise that on Yahweh's arrival the wicked will be burned like stubble (Mal. 3.19).

All four of these collections rely on a sharp demarcation between 'us' and 'them'. In Habakkuk, Zechariah 9, and Zechariah 12, 'them' is the nations: Habakkuk protests the wickedness of the Chaldeans, and Zechariah 9 denounces the cities of Syria and Philistia. Zechariah 12, however, most sharply distinguishes Judah from 'all the nations of the earth' (12.3), envisioning a time in which Jerusalem will become the cup of reeling for the nations, a heavy stone (though a different Hebrew word, it bears an evocative connection to the 'heaviness' of *maśśā'*) that will harm all who try to dislodge it, a flaming torch that will devour the nations. The inhabitants of Jerusalem, in contrast, will receive Yahweh's compassion.

Malachi stands out from the other texts in this regard. While the book begins with a concern about a foreign nation, claiming that the destruction of Edom proves that Yahweh favors Jacob (the ancestor of Judah) over Esau (the ancestor of Edom), the nations do not figure elsewhere in Malachi's message. Rather, the book directs judgment toward Judah's own people and priests; the wicked and the righteous that it sharply distinguishes (especially in ch. 3) are both within 'us'.

2. *Isaiah 13–23, Oracles against the Nations*. The use of the term *maśśā'* to describe a prophetic unit is used frequently in Isaiah 13–23, appearing at 13.1; 15.1; 17.1; 19.1; 21.1, 11, 13; 22.1; 23.1; and 30.6. The genre of this material is often designated as Oracles against the Nations (OAN), a term usually reserved for extended diatribes, even though other prophetic material (as we saw above) can address judgment to those outside Judah. The OAN do not follow a standard form, and not all begin with *maśśā'*. The Isaianic collection at hand is noteworthy in that it is both a *maśśā'* text and an OAN, a distinction that is shared with Nahum.

A close reading highlights numerous intriguing intertextual connections between Nahum and Isaiah 13–23. For example, a reader might compare the theophany in Isaiah 13 with Nah. 1.2-8; the fate of children in Isa. 13.16-18 with Nah. 3.10-13; as well as the personification of the enemy nation as a woman in Isaiah 17 with Nahum 3. Of greater significance for a reading of Nahum, however, are the overarching themes of Isaiah 13–23.

As Erlandsson (1970: 102) outlines, those foreign nations that are singled out for inclusion in Isaiah 13–23 all bear a close connection to Assyria: all have already been defeated by Assyria, are on the verge of being defeated by Assyria, or belong to anti-Assyrian coalitions. In addition, Erlandsson (1970: 103) maintains, 'The threads which bind together 14.24–23.18 are primarily 1) Assyria's behavior; 2) the attempts through a policy of alliances to crush Assyria; and 3) the proclamation that it is Yahweh who will crush Assyria and guarantee Zion's security'.

This last feature is worthy of particular note. As in the general prophetic materials against foreign nations, here too in Isaiah 13–23 the defeat of Assyria is intimately connected with salvation for Judah. Isaiah 13–23 underscores the agent of this salvation; according to Erlandsson

(1970: 103): 'It is also part of Yahweh's design to guarantee Zion's security, wherefore it is from Yahweh that the people shall seek help against the aggressors... Assyria shall fall by a sword, but not of man (Isa. 31.8)'.

3. *Reading Nahum as a* maśśāʾ *text: some observations.* The intertextual effects of Nahum's categorization as a *maśśāʾ* are significant. Primarily, such a labeling narrows interpretative options. While prophetic books in general may contain various combinations of announcements of judgment and salvation (including announcements of judgment to the community itself), *maśśāʾ* texts tend to restrict themselves to judgment for others and salvation for us. All *maśśāʾ* texts are characterized by a strong dichotomy between us and them: the wicked stand opposed to the righteous (Hab. 1.4; Mal. 3.18), and the nations stand opposed to Jerusalem (Zech. 9; 12). In turn, judgment of the nations is by definition salvation for Israel and/or Judah. The label *maśśāʾ*, then, invokes a literary world in which punishment for the wicked is necessary for the salvation of the righteous, and it clues its reader to expect harsh words for 'them' and promises of salvation for 'us'. Connections with Isaiah 13–23 also evoke Assyrian settings.

B. Nineveh

I argued in the Introduction for a literary understanding of Nahum's references to Nineveh: 'the literariness of the prophetic traditions remains whatever evaluation we may make of their historical reliability, and it is as literature that they must be interpreted' (Carroll 1988: 31). Here I would like to explore the 'literariness' of Nineveh in the book of Nahum. What effect on reading Nahum does the mention of Nineveh have? What images in a reader's mind does 'Nineveh' evoke? How do Nineveh and/or Assyria intertexts guide our reading of Nahum?

Throughout the biblical materials, Nineveh/Assyria is cast as the enemy of Israel and Judah. By attributing the building of Nineveh to Nimrod, a descendant of Ham, Genesis's Table of Nations marks the city as genealogical Other (the terms 'land of Assyria' and 'land of Nimrod' are used synonymously in Mic. 5.6). 2 Kings describes the aggression of the Assyrian military against Israel and Judah; and the Deuteronomistic History and the prophetic literature underscore the cruelty of Assyria, both for its destruction of the northern kingdom and for its political and military control of Judah during the eighth and seventh centuries BCE.

Assyria nowhere receives so much attention as in the book of Isaiah, where it features prominently both as Yahweh's enemy and as Yahweh's tool for punishing Judah. I will focus below on the destabilizing effect that this latter affirmation of Isaiah has on a reading of Nahum, but for our present purposes appreciating the weight of Assyria in the book of Isaiah is crucial. Isaiah insists that Assyria's successes and failures are determined not by its own strategies and power but rather by the purposes of Yahweh. In Isaiah, Assyria's fortunes become the barometer of Yahweh's relationship with Judah: when Judah is rebellious, Assyria prevails (Isa. 10); when Judah and its leaders repent and turn to Yahweh, then Assyria falls (Isa. 37).

In Isaiah, as well as in other prophetic literature, the mention of Assyria is often paired with that of Egypt (Isa. 7.18; 11.11; 19.23-25; 20.4; 27.13; Hos. 7.11; 9.3; 11.5, 11; 12.1; Mic. 7.12; Zech. 10.10, 11). While this pairing likely reflects the geopolitical realities of the eighth century, in these materials Assyria and Egypt represent the ultimate powers of the world, the standards against which might is assessed:

> On that day there will be a highway from Egypt to Assyria, and the Assyrian will come into Egypt, and the Egyptian into Assyria, and the Egyptians will worship with the Assyrians. On that day Israel will be the third with Egypt and Assyria, a blessing in the midst of the earth (Isa. 19.23-24).

While Assyria/Nineveh functions within the biblical material as 'ultimate enemy', it does not become a mere symbol for evil. Unlike the Nahum Pesher from Qumran in which Assyria loses it historical particularity and becomes the symbol of all that oppresses the faithful, the biblical materials remember Assyria as a concrete, formidable foe—a remembered trauma of the nation's past. For example, in discussing the fate of Judah in the Babylonian period, Jer. 50.17 and Ezekiel 23 recall the fate of Israel under the Assyrians; and even the 'historical fictions' of Jonah and Tobit are set in Assyria to evoke not the image of 'Everyplace' but of a concrete, albeit ancient, enemy.

By calling itself a *maśśā'* against Nineveh, Nahum's superscription invokes Nineveh not as a past kingdom but as a present reality. Whenever the book was written, the superscription instructs its reader to interpret what follows within the Assyrian period. It is the implied historical setting for this piece of literature. Given the unflattering characterization of Assyria in the biblical intertexts, such an implied setting predisposes a reader to imagine that the community is currently threatened by a brutal foe. Moreover, read alongside Isaiah, which draws an inverse correlation between Assyria's fate and that of Israel and/or Judah, Nahum's superscription also raises the possibility that what follows is good news for Judah. If Assyria is being punished, then Yahweh's intentions toward Judah must be good.

C. A Book of a Vision

On first reading, it appears ironic that the only prophetic collection called a book also is described as the result of a vision ($h^azôn$)—a seeming contradiction of media—yet much of the prophetic literature portrays itself as a written version of what a prophet has perceived by the eye or the ear. The frequent use of prophetic messenger speech, 'thus says Yahweh', reinforces that perception, as does the frequent use of the term 'vision' to characterize what the prophets proclaim.

$H^azôn$ appears in the Hebrew Bible almost exclusively to refer to prophecy; its only other reference is to a 'night vision' (Isa. 29.7). Isaiah and Obadiah are also labeled visions in their superscriptions, and 2 Chron. 32.32 calls the book of Isaiah the 'vision of Isaiah'. The superscriptions of Amos, Micah and Habakkuk (the latter, like Nahum, is also called a *massā'*) refer to what the prophet 'saw', using the related verbal form *hazâ*.

$H^azôn$ refers not simply to data registered by the eyes but rather to truth made known by Yahweh, as Jer. 23.16 makes clear: 'They [false prophets] speak visions of their own minds, not from the mouth of Yahweh.' In apocalyptic contexts, where $h^azôn$ is especially prevalent (it appears 11 times in the book of Daniel), it implies an ecstatic vision of the heavenly realm.

The designation of the material to follow as a vision casts the prophetic speaker as a passive recipient of a divine message, a reporter rather than an author. Such a stance, according to Jones (1996: 75) who discerns it in the *massā'* genre as well,

> has the rhetorical effect of unobtrusively promoting the speaker's implicit arguments while maintaining the appearance of objectivity. It is as if he speaks from the point of view of the audience, and by speaking from this perspective 'the rhetor makes his audience's point-of-view congruent with his own. The audience looks over the rhetor's shoulder and watches the event unfold from the same angle of vision. Alignment of perspective encourages alignment of belief (quoting Fox 1980: 8-9).

Importantly, however, Nahum is identified not as the vision itself but as a *sēper* of the vision. The usual English translation as 'book' implies one particular technology of collecting writing materials: a bound collection of loose pages, properly termed a codex. The Hebrew term *sēper* does not carry the same set of associations. In the Hebrew Bible it refers to any written document, including a letter; the codex form did not appear until a much later period.

Although other prophetic materials are linked with writing (Jer. 36.2; Hab. 2.2; Ezek. 3), no other prophetic superscription identifies the material to follow as a *sēper*. Such an identification not only demonstrates that, as R. Smith (1984: 71) suggests, 'Nahum is self-consciously a piece of literature', but also it sets reading boundaries. Authority resides not in the vision itself, not in the experience of a prophet named Nahum, but in the words and letters bounded by the beginning and ending of these particular words: 'Herewith, meaning is to be produced in writing' (Said 1985: 59). The reader is invited to know divine will not through his or her own experience or vision but through reading the words of this book.

D. Nahum the Elkoshite

The name Nahum may either be a noun meaning 'comfort' or a shortened form of Nehemiah, 'Yahweh has given comfort'. While a common west-Semitic name, it appears in this form nowhere else in the Hebrew Bible. The only information given about Nahum is that he is 'Elkoshi', that is, one from the town of Elkosh, a town of unknown origin. The arguments by which some scholars locate the city in Galilee, in southwestern Judah, or even near Nineveh, rest solely on inferences from the book itself. Hence, while there may have been a Nahum the Elkoshite, the prophet remains anonymous to us, inviting us to consider the literary effect of his connection with the book.

The use of a personal name in the superscription confirms earlier perceptions that Nahum should be categorized as a prophetic book. Amos and Jeremiah are similarly identified by their hometowns, though Micah's superscription most resembles that of Nahum ('Micah the Moreshite', Mic. 1.1). The author-izing of the book, in turn, activates the reading memory of the 'prophetic' themes that we have already encountered—issues of authority, temporality, historicity. That Nahum is mentioned in connection with Nineveh further invites us to consider him as a real prophet who spoke in the period of Assyrian hegemony, much as Isaiah did.

Most commentators draw no connection between this personal name and the message of the book, treating as ironic or even nonsensical the connection between 'comfort' and the book's vengeance-filled contents. The literary worlds of the OAN and the *maśśā'*, however, draw clear connections between devastation of the enemy and the comfort of Judah, forging a fit between the allusions of Nahum's name and the world view of this book. In much the same way, Isaiah 40 opens with an announcement of 'comfort' following the harsh words and concern with Assyria that fill Isaiah 1–39.

Similarly, the designation 'Elkoshi' may be a literary play on the themes of Nahum. It is comprised of two elements: *'el*, 'God'; and *qāšâ*, 'hard', the same root used throughout Exodus to describe the 'hardening' of Pharaoh's heart. The precise nuance of 'Elkoshi' cannot be defined ('The one whom God makes hard'? 'The one who makes God hard'? 'God of my hardness'?), but its etymology is evocative in such a 'hard', 'burdensome' book.

E. Effects of the Details: Some Observations

In its choice to begin with these particular details, as well as with a prophetic superscription in general, the book of Nahum instructs us how to read what follows. This book is to be read as (a) divine speech; (b) delivered through an historical individual; (c) in the Assyrian period; (d) against the Assyrians; (e) who were cruel oppressors. The fact that Assyria did indeed fall, known through intertextual readings of the Deuteronomistic History, also raises the possibility of a causal connection between Nahum's words against Assyria and its ultimate fate. Perhaps Nahum's words are not merely a hope, a wish, but indeed a performative imprecation.

III. Postscript: The Problems with Beginnings

> There is always the danger of too much reflection upon beginnings (Said 1985: 76).

In my discussion so far, I have considered how Nahum's intertexts, particularly Isaiah and other prophetic voices, guide the reader to the conclusions I have just summarized. As I noted in the Introduction, however, intertextual readings also problematize the creation of meaning; according to Kristeva, the synchronous reading of multiple texts undermines the meaning of any given one (for an application of Kristeva to biblical studies, see Beal 1997).

This destabilizing effect of intertextuality is most clearly seen in the simultaneous reading of Nahum and the book of Isaiah. Earlier I indicated that, when read in conjunction, Nahum and Isaiah 13–23 collude to paint Assyria as an evil enemy, a nation whose punishment extends to all who align themselves with it. And yet, the book of Isaiah's larger vision of Assyria destabilizes that simple conclusion. Isaiah insists that the impending success of the Assyrians is Yahweh's means of punishing Judah for its own sin: Assyrian success is Judah's own fault. Hence, while the *maśśā'* form announces a reversal of fortunes (the enemy is about to be routed and we are about to be saved), Isaiah's affirmation calls attention to the question that remains unasked in Nahum: what was *our* sin that allowed the enemy to succeed in the first place? Are 'we' and 'they' so easily distinguished if we have been wicked, too? An intertextual reading of Nahum with Malachi similarly reminds the reader that 'we' are not monolithic. The wicked can be members of the community itself.

Chart 1: *Prophetic superscriptions compared*

Prophet	Vehicle of Inspiration	Family Information	Locale
Isaiah	vision of Isaiah which he saw	son of Amoz	
Jeremiah	words of Jeremiah to whom the word of Yahweh came	son of Hilkiah from the priests who were in Anathoth in land of Benjamin	
Ezekiel	I saw visions of God; the word of Yahweh was to Ezekiel; the hand of Yahweh	son of Buzi	among the exiles by the river Chebar
Hosea	word of Yahweh which was to Hosea	son of Beeri	
Joel	word of Yahweh which was to Joel	son of Pethuel	
Amos	words of Amos; which he saw		who was among the shepherds in Tekoa
Obadiah	the vision of Obadiah		
Jonah	word of Yahweh was to Jonah	son of Ammitai	
Micah	word of Yahweh which was to Micah; which he saw	the Moreshite	
Nahum	oracle; book of the vision of Nahum	the Elkoshite	
Habakkuk	oracle that Habakkuk saw		
Zephaniah	word of Yahweh was to Zephaniah	son of Cushi son of Gedaliah son of Amariah son of Hezekiah	
Haggai	the word of Yahweh by the hand of Haggai		
Zechariah	the word of Yahweh to Zechariah	son of Berechiah son of Iddo	
Malachi	oracle; word of Yahweh by the hand of Malachi		

Political Setting	Target/Recipient	Other Information
in the days of King Uzziah of Judah and in the days of King Jeroboam son of Joash of Israel	concerning Judah and Jerusalem	
in the days of King Josiah son of Amon of Judah, in the 13th year of his reign; also in the days of King Jehoiakim son of Josiah of Judah, and until the end of the 11th year of King Zedekiah son of Josiah of Judah, until the captivity of Jerusalem in the 5th month.		
in the 30th year, in the 4th month, on the 5th day of the month; the 5th day of the month (5th year of the exile of King Jehoiachin)		priest
in the days of Kings Uzziah, Jotham, Ahaz, and Hezekiah of Judah, and in the days of King Jeroboam son of Joash of Israel		
in the days of King Uzziah of Judah and in the days of King Jeroboam son of Joash of Israel	against Israel	two years before the earthquake
in the days of Kings Jotham, Ahaz, and Hezekiah of Judah	concerning Samaria and Jerusalem	
	of Nineveh	
		the prophet
in the days of King Josiah son of Amon of Judah		
In the second year of King Darius, in the 6th month, on the 1st day of the month	to Zerubbabel son of Shealtiel, governor of Judah, and to Joshua son of Jehozadak, the high priest	the prophet
In the 8th month, in the 2nd year of Darius		the prophet
	to Israel	

I also highlight the tension inherent in the phrase 'the book of a vision'. While the designation of Nahum as a *sēper* attempts to restrict the divine word to the parameters of the book, the recognition that its ultimate authority derives from its visionary character works against such containment. Other visions are always possible, waiting to spoil the boundaries and authority of this book.

In addition, the book's designation as a *sēper* suggests something of the material conditions of its production. To be written, a book needs a writer and a reader, skills that privilege some and not others. Its very attempts to author-ize itself through attribution to an unknown person from an unknown town betray the book's failure to name its agent. Who wrote this book? For whom? Why?

Despite the book's self-labeling as authoritative divine speech, not all readers (historical or contemporary) have read it as such, instead attributing its attitudes to the very human Nahum or to a nationalistic sentiment. Is there anything about the book itself that allows the reader to resist the framing function of the superscription? This is a question I shall continue to explore, as we consider the rest of the book and how it bears the burden of its superscription.

Nahum 1.2-10

> Wrath is cruel, anger is overwhelming, but who is able to stand before jealousy? (Prov. 27.4)

The generic labels and other details of Nahum's superscription have suggested to the reader that this book will be directed against the Other: it is *Nineveh*'s burden to bear. This unit, however, does not address—or even mention— Nineveh, but rather turns to a bold description of Yahweh, *Judah*'s God.

I. The Unit

The organization of the book, including the beginning and ending of individual units, has engendered substantial debate. Many scholars treat 1.2-8 as an independent unit, based on the argument that these verses comprise a partial alphabetic acrostic, the lines beginning successively with the first 11 letters of the Hebrew alphabet. Advanced since at least the nineteenth century, this theory has formed so great a consensus that the most popular modern Hebrew Bible, the *BHS*, prints the alphabetic sequence in the margin of the text. Some scholars have extended the theory, attempting to trace the continuation of the acrostic into ch. 2.

If indeed present, an alphabetic acrostic would serve as further indication of the 'literariness' of the book and would collude with the rhetoric of the superscription's designation of Nahum as a *sēper* in privileging reading over hearing. I find Floyd's (1994) arguments *against* the acrostic, however, compelling: to maintain the alphabetic sequence one must propose lines of very different lengths, emend the text, and, most importantly, ignore the way in which 1.9-10 fits into the section's larger argument. Floyd well demonstrates the structural coherence of 1.2-10—how both 1.6 and 1.9 follow general descriptions with rhetorical questions and how 1.11 signals a new unit by a change in addressee.

II. The Inner World of 1.2-10

A. Reading 1.2-10

Read alone, apart from the superscription, 1.2-10 finds no anchor in time or place. Rather, it begins its characterization of Yahweh by recounting his enduring characteristics (my use of masculine language reflecting Nahum's consistent characterization of Yahweh as male). The literary style of 1.2-3a speaks of the present and the permanent, rather

than of the past or the occasional. Nahum 1.2 employs present participles throughout: Yahweh is 'the jealous one', the vengeful one', 'the
one who rages'. In 1.3a, adjectives perform the same durative function:
'Yahweh [is] slow of anger, and [is] great of strength'. The one verbal
form ('he will indeed not acquit', 1.3a) is imperfect, that mood in
Hebrew reserved for incomplete, and often continuing, action. Style
indicates that these are features of the deity which do not change.

A series of literary techniques focuses the reader's attention on one of
these characteristics of Yahweh—his vengeance. The first and most
obvious technique is that of repetition. The phrase 'the vengeful one [is]
Yahweh' appears three times in 1.2; while other personality traits are
named, vengeance remains structurally and topically the center of the
verse.

Allusion also focuses the reader's attention on Yahweh's vengeance.
Nahum 1.2-3 quotes the most frequent and fundamental characterization
of Yahweh in the Hebrew Bible. Found in Num. 14.18; Joel 2.13; Jon.
4.2; Ps. 86.15; 103.8; 145.8 and Neh. 9.17 as well, its classic formulation
appears in Exod. 34.6-7:

A comparison of the Exodus passage with that of Nahum calls
attention to Nahum's divergence from the standard refrain:

Exod. 34.6-7	Nah. 1.2-3
Yahweh, Yahweh, a God merciful and gracious, slow to anger, and abounding in steadfast love and faithfulness, keeping steadfast love for the thousandth generation, forgiving iniquity and transgression and sin, yet by no means clearing the guilty, but visiting the iniquity of the parents upon the children and the children's children, to the third and the fourth generation.	A jealous and avenging God is Yahweh, Yahweh is avenging and wrathful; Yahweh takes vengeance on his adversaries and rages against his enemies. Yahweh is slow to anger but great in power, and Yahweh will by no means clear the guilty. His way is in whirlwind and storm, and the clouds are the dust of his feet.

While both Exodus and Nahum agree that the deity is slow to anger and
that he avenges, the structure of Nah. 1.2 clearly prioritizes Yahweh's
vengeance.

In the Hebrew Bible, vengeance (*nāqām*) refers both to human and to
divine activity but, while human vengeance is variously treated as
acceptable (e.g. Exod. 21.20) and as vindictive (e.g. Ezek. 25.12, 15; also
see Pitard 1992: 786), divine vengeance is always accorded positive
weight. Vengeance is Yahweh's righting of wrongs, invoked in appeals
for justice.

> But you, Yahweh of hosts, who judge righteously, who try the heart and the mind, let me see your retribution upon them, for to you I have committed my cause (Jer. 11.20).

Nahum only gradually reveals *against whom* this divine vengeance is directed, building the reader's suspense. Not until the third stanza of 1.2 does the reader learn that the thrice-repeated vengefulness of Yahweh is directed against his enemies. The insistence in 1.3a that Yahweh is also great of power indicates further that Yahweh's temperament can be translated into (devastating) action.

The focus on Yahweh's vengefulness continues throughout the unit, as the general description of Yahweh in 1.2-3a gives way to an awesome portrait of Yahweh the Divine Warrior in 1.3b-8. Texts that describe the deity as a conquering Warrior appear frequently in the Hebrew Bible, drawing on common vocabulary and ideology (e.g. Judg. 5; 2 Sam. 22; Ps. 18; Hab. 3; Amos 1; Isa. 29). The proposed origin of this motif in ancient Near Eastern cosmological myths may account for its use of nature imagery: like Baal, the Canaanite god of thunder, Yahweh appears as a storm, lightning flashing, thunder rocking the earth; as in Canaanite and Babylonian myths, the forces of chaos appear in the guise of a monster or of the sea.

The Divine Warrior texts rely on the conviction that Yahweh's vengeance is warranted and just, a righting of wrongs. As discussed above, *maśśā'* texts often include a theophany of the Divine Warrior as a response to cries against injustice:

> You came forth to save your people, to save your anointed. You crushed the head of the wicked house, laying it bare from foundation to roof... I wait quietly for the day of calamity to come upon the people who attack us (Hab. 3.13).

This connection of Divine Warrior and just vengeance is not limited to *maśśā'* texts. Numerous biblical passages describe Yahweh as vindicating his own people by crushing their/his enemies:

> Praise, O heavens, his people, worship him, all you gods! For he will avenge the blood of his children, and take vengeance on his adversaries; he will repay those who hate him, and cleanse the land for his people (Deut. 32.43).

> The righteous will rejoice when they see vengeance done; they will bathe their feet in the blood of the wicked (Ps. 58.10).

In yet other biblical texts, particularly prophetic ones, the Divine Warrior marches against the community itself. Micah opens with Yahweh thundering out of his place to confront Judah: 'All this is for the transgression of Jacob and for the sins of the house of Israel' (Mic. 1.5). Similarly, the judgment of Judah in Amos is enveloped by the opening theophany in 1.2 and the vision of Yahweh the Warrior in 9.1-10. Isaiah, the book most closely intertextually related with Nahum, envisions Judah's destruction at the hand of the Warrior (Isa. 5; 9; 29) as the just punishment for its crimes—Yahweh the bloodstained warrior fighting both against his own people and against their foes (Isa. 63). Confronted with the overwhelming, awesome power of the deity in Nah. 1.2-5, the reader can only understand 1.6 as a rhetorical question. No one— neither the enemy nor the friend—can withstand this deity, especially when he is angry.

On first reading, Nah. 1.7 seems a *non sequitur*. A Yahweh who instills such fear, whose anger threatens the very earth and all who dwell within it (1.5), is now affirmed as 'good'? In the rhetorical world of the Divine Warrior texts, however, the deity's ability and willingness to act in decisive ways *is* the hallmark of goodness. Especially in those texts in which Yahweh vindicates Judah against its enemies, divine retribution is the sign of Yahweh's care. The contrast between Yahweh's vengeance against enemies and his care for his own people is underscored by the end of 1.7 where, as throughout the Psalms, 'those who take refuge' stands as the antonym for 'enemies':

> Wondrously show your steadfast love, O savior of those who seek refuge from their adversaries at your right hand (Ps. 17.7).

> Yahweh helps them and rescues them; he rescues them from the wicked, and saves them, because they take refuge in him (Ps. 37.40).

Nahum 1.8 is difficult, if not impossible, to translate. Literally, it may be rendered 'in a flood overflowing an end he will make, her place, and his enemies he will pursue darkness'. What 'place' is this, and to whom does 'her' refer?' Attempting to read with the MT, ASV gives 'he will make a full end of her place'; related translations are NAS ('its site') and NJV ('its place'). NIV assumes that 'her place' refers to Nineveh and adds the proper name to the text, in keeping with the logic of Roberts (1991: 71-72) and Spronk (1997: 49-50). Both RSV and NRSV follow the Septuagint and read 'he will make a full end to his adversaries'. Other attempts to render sense to the verse include those of Cathcart (1973: 57), who revocalizes 'her place' to read 'hostilities or enemies'; Coggins (1985: 26), who ignores the suffix and posits that 'place' refers to the Temple; Floyd (2000: 36), who connects the feminine suffix to the last mentioned feminine noun—'adversity' in 1.7a—and NAB, which reads 'all those who defy him'.

All these translations, however, ignore the syntax of the phrase 'he will make an end' in its other occurrences in the Hebrew Bible. When used with an object, the verb takes a 'helping' preposition. Just as in English one makes an end 'of' or 'to' something, so too in Hebrew 'make an end' requires the prepositions *'et* (Jer. 5.18; 46.28; Ezek. 11.13; 20.17; Zeph. 1.18) or *b* (Jer. 30.11). In cases in which the phrase appears without a preposition (Isa. 10.23; Neh. 9.31) it takes no object. The difficulty of translating Nah. 1.8 is further complicated by the fact that the same phrase appears in 1.9 without an object. The repetition of the phrase is often considered a sign of scribal error.

In keeping with the project of this commentary to read Nahum in its final form from a literary perspective, my question remains, 'what does reading 1.8 in its final form (in the MT) do to a reader?' I see two viable responses: (1) 'her' is proleptic, referring ahead to the feminine noun 'adversary' in 1.9; or (2) 'her place' is an enigma, a phrase out of place, without sense. Indeed, I shall suggest that throughout Nahum, dangling pronouns leave the reader puzzled, off guard.

The imagery of 1.8 is clearer than its translation. 'The flood' represents unstoppable devastation, as in Dan. 9.26 and 11.10, the latter close in wording to Nahum: 'the troops of the prince who is to come shall destroy the city and the sanctuary. Its end shall come with a flood, and to the end there shall be war' (Dan. 9.26). Numerous Divine Warrior texts, including Jer. 47.2, also describe devastation as a flood.

A problem that will demand much of our attention in 1.11-14 first surfaces in 1.9. Whom is Nahum addressing as 'you', here in the masculine plural? On the one hand, similarities in style and content suggest that 1.9 is to be understood along the lines of 1.6, as a rhetorical question underscoring the futility of resisting Yahweh: 'you' in 1.9 may be as general as 'who' in 1.6. On the other hand, 1.9 has introduced something new in Nahum. It marks the first time in the book that anyone has been addressed directly.

Appreciating the literary features of 1.10 comes more easily than the verse's translation. Literally reading 'like unto intertwined thorns and like their drinking, drunkards, (they are) eaten up like chaff dry full', the verse is highly alliterative, in Hebrew full of s, b, and k sounds (*sᵉbukîm ûkᵉsobᵉʾām sᵉbûʾîm*). Intertwining two divergent similes—that of knotted thorns and drunkards—the verse, like the images it employs, twists and staggers (perhaps in an attempt to render greater coherence, both NAB and NJB omit any reference to drunkenness.)

Intrigued and confused by the concatenation of similes, a reader could forget to ask to whom 'they' (the ones who are like drunks and thorns, consumed like chaff) refers? Are 'they' the 'enemies' of 1.8, or persons yet unnamed? For the third time in the unit (1.8, 'her place'; 1.9, 'you';

1.10, 'they'), the reader has witnessed Yahweh's anger against an unclearly identified target.

B. Concluding Observations about the Inner World of 1.2-10

Yahweh's character is revealed in this opening section of Nahum through the contrast between his treatment of his friends and of his enemies. Yahweh is vengeful toward and rages against his enemies (1.2); he is a place of safety for those who take refuge in him (1.7); and he pursues his enemies into darkness (1.8). Read in light of other Divine Warrior texts, Nahum suggests that this discrimination response arises from Yahweh's justice: Yahweh's revenge is the appropriate response to wrongdoing.

The unit itself offers no indication as to whether the reader is to iden-tify with Yahweh's friend or Yahweh's foe. Yahweh is called 'good' in 1.7, but by a detached narrator, one who does not necessarily share the per-spective of the reader. Given that other prophetic books consider the Divine Warrior's action against his own people as a sign of his justice, the reader is not yet invited to assume that 'good' means 'good for me'.

Employment of the Divine Warrior motif does, however, lead the reader to believe that wrongdoing has precipitated the theophany here described. If Yahweh appears to avenge wrongdoing, what wrong has been done? And, more importantly, who has done it?

III. Reading 1.2-10 with the Superscription

On one level, reading 1.2-10 in conjunction with the superscription answers these very questions. Via its description of what follows as a *maśśā'* against Nineveh, that ultimately evil nation, the superscription leads the reader to identify the enemy in 1.2-10 as Assyria. That identi-fication has yet further effects: the reader (who is Not-Nineveh) is invited to identify with 'those who take refuge in Yahweh' and to read the goodness of Yahweh in 1.7 as 'goodness for me'. Such an identification further solidifies the equation between 'Yahweh's enemies' and 'my enemies'.

Not only does 1.1 carry forward into an understanding of 1.2-10, com-forting the reader into believing that he or she knows who Yahweh's enemies are, but also 1.2-10 bleeds backward into the superscription, altering the perception of Nineveh. The mythological nature of the Divine Warrior poem suggests that Nineveh is not only a formidable military foe of Judah but also, more importantly, a suprahistorical enemy of Yahweh, one who threatens the cosmic order. Scholars who see 1.2-10 as universalizing Nahum's message, an editorial addition intended to broaden the significance beyond the historical vicissitudes of the Assyrian period (e.g. Marks 1987: 216-17), can do so only by ignoring the superscription. When 1.1-10 is read sequentially, Nineveh does not become a general signifier for all forces that work against Yahweh; rather, the historically specific Nineveh is demonized as the cosmic enemy of Yahweh.

IV. A Controlling Superscription?

The ability of Nah. 1.1-10 to create such a world view in the reader is dependent on its ability to keep its categories clear. The fates of Yahweh's enemies and Yahweh's friends must remain distinct in order for Yahweh to be shown as just. If Nineveh is the enemy (1.1), then Yahweh's wrath must be directed to it. As Not-Nineveh, the reader must, then, be Yahweh's friend and find Yahweh as a place of safety (1.7).

Several features of 1.2-10 destabilize this dichotomy. The use of present participles in 1.2 suggests that vengeance is a permanent attribute of Yahweh. In 1.2, Yahweh is twice called vengeful as a free-floating, unbounded characteristic; only on the third stanza of the affirmation is Yahweh's vengeance limited to his enemies.

Yet more destabilizing to Nahum's dichotomies is the lack of pronoun antecedents in 1.8-10. How can I rest assured that Yahweh is a place of safety for me if I cannot identify whose 'place' will come to an end (1.8) or the 'they' who will be burned like dry chaff? In this familiar, and supposedly comforting, picture of a Yahweh who will protect me from his/my enemies, why am I being warned not to plot against Yahweh (1.9)? Why am I addressed at all? Is not this book against Nineveh?

In addition, intertexts not only bolster but also trouble my reading of this book as solely against Nineveh. *Maśśā'* texts can be directed against me as well as them, as the case of Malachi shows. In prophetic Divine Warrior texts, Yahweh marches against Judah as often as he marches against other nations, and he can fight against both in a single battle (Isa. 63).

What does the reader learn about Yahweh in reading Nah. 1.1-10? I have learned that Yahweh can and will devastate his enemies and provide safety to those who take refuge in him. But because I do not know how to determine into which category I fall at any given time, I have first and foremost learned to fear Yahweh.

Nahum 1.11-14

The characterization of Yahweh having been completed in the prior unit, 1.11-14 turns to direct address and prophetic announcement. Here, we learn not of Yahweh's permanent characteristics but rather of his specific intentions for the current situation. And yet, those affected by the grave events about to take place are left unnamed, marked only by pronouns that shift in gender and number, lacking clear antecedents. To whom and about whom is Nahum speaking?

I. Reading 1.11-14

The lack of pronominal antecedents that will plague the unit begins immediately in 1.11. Who is 'you'?

One clue is grammatical: 'you' in 1.11 is feminine singular. The contextual clues provided by the rest of the verse, however, are themselves contested. Most English Bibles translate the verb that follows with some variation of 'come out' or 'come forth', implying that 'you' is the origin and accomplice of a 'plotter'—a term marked as negative by similar usage in 1.9 and by its parallelism with 'counselor of perversity'. If indeed the (evil) plotter is one of 'you', then the verse is accusatory, blaming 'you' for the actions of one in its midst. Among the scholars who read the verse in this manner, some claim that it judges Judah, who will be addressed in 2.1 in the feminine; others trace the antecedent of 'you' back to the superscription, where (evil) Nineveh is feminine. In keeping with this second option, NIV supplements the text to read 'you, O Nineveh' (as in Nah. 1.8).

In Hebrew, the verb translated as 'come out' also can mean 'depart from'. Hence, the verse may not be accusatory at all but rather a recounting of something positive that happened in the past: 'from you an evil plotter departed'. The perfect tense of the verb indicates completed action—a nuance obscured by the tendency of translations to render the verb in the English present perfect. Floyd (2000: 50-51), who reads 1.11 as recounting an historical event, suggests that Yahweh is reminding the community of the departure of Sennacherib from the gates of Jerusalem in 701, seen in Isaiah 37 as Yahweh's gracious response to King Hezekiah's prayer.

Prophetic messenger speech ('thus says Yahweh') appears for the first time in Nahum in 1.12; for the first time, Yahweh is named as speaker.

But in contrast to the usual pattern, messenger speech is not immediately followed by an announcement about the future. Focus remains temporarily on the past ('though they were strong and numerous, they were cut off and passed'). Most English translations render these verbs in the future tense ('they shall be cut off and pass away'), either ignoring the perfect tense or relying on the somewhat dated theory that the prophets speak in a 'prophetic perfect', so assured of the outcome of their pronouncements that they can describe it as already accomplished.

Even more crucial than the 'when' of these events is the 'who'. To whom does 'they' in 1.12 refer? Like the 'plotter' of 1.11, 'they' are opposed to Yahweh; but if the same enemy is described, then why the shift to the masculine plural? Floyd sees the variation as 'indiscriminate' and not particularly important (Floyd 2000: 48). This 'unimportant' variation occurs not only between verses but within them: in 1.12, 'they shall be cut off' is plural, but 'pass away' is singular.

Nahum 1.12b presents the reader with new, weighty information. In a single Hebrew word, Yahweh reveals that he himself is responsible for the addressee's current suffering: 'I afflicted you' (feminine singular, as in 1.11). Nahum's intertexts, especially those from Isaiah, have always kept Judah's accountability for Assyrian oppression on the edge of the reader's consciousness, but Nahum itself has not before this point explicitly claimed Yahweh's complicity in Assyrian hegemony.

Before the reader can absorb this admission and its implications for reassessing Yahweh's relationship to his friends, new information supersedes it. Speaking in the future tense (technically, the imperfect, used for any uncompleted action), Yahweh proclaims, 'I will not afflict you anymore'. The promise of a positive future, contrasted with an oppressive present, continues into 1.13: 'I will break his (masculine singular) yoke from upon you (feminine singular)'.

To this point in the unit, the pronouns without antecedents have been employed in a fairly consistent manner. The feminine singular character, promised impending salvation from an enemy whose success is attributable to Yahweh, has been addressed in the second person. The enemy has been described in the third person and as masculine, although the alternation of singular and plural allows the reader to imagine either a single enemy described in two ways or a coalition of male enemies. Nahum 1.14 breaks the pattern. The 'you' now addressed is masculine singular, and the announcement is that of punishment. These changes lead the reader to believe that someone new is being addressed, but, as before, the identity remains obscure. Floyd suggests that the three threats—loss of procreation, loss of idols, and preparation of a grave— suggest a royal figure, making the 'you' of 1.14 a foreign king (Floyd

2000: 49). The unit itself, however, provides little basis for such an identification.

II. Reading 1.11-14 with 1.1-10

This unit draws a sharp contrast between the punishment that awaits one figure and the salvation that is promised for another. By refusing to name *who* will meet such divergent fates, the text leaves the reader anxious, and sets him or her to sifting for clues among all that the book has already revealed. Seeking to fill the interpretative gaps left by 1.11-14, the reader rereads all that has come before.

The affirmation of the superscription takes on new weight in light of the questions that 1.11-14 raises. Lest the reader forget who he or she is and on what side he or she belongs, the book proclaims itself as a *maśśā'* against Nineveh, speech that addresses the Other. The superscription relieves the discomfort of 1.11-14. This is a book against Nineveh, not against me. As a label, a categorization, the superscription overshadows inconsistencies. Even though the enemy is masculine (1.11-14) and Nineveh is feminine (1.1), an enemy remains an enemy.

The superscription's insistence that the enemy is Nineveh grants probability to Floyd's suggestion that 1.14 addresses the Assyrian king. While other, average persons also would find the loss of progeny, desecration of religious symbols, and the creation of a grave threatening, who more logically than the king stands as a singular representative for his plural nation? With the superscription as an anchor, a reader could assume that the rod that is broken in 1.13 is that of the king of Assyria and that 'they' who are numerous (1.12) and like tangled thorns and staggering drunkards (1.10) are the Assyrians themselves. Yet such an identification of 'he' with the king of Assyria is only suggested. Nahum has not yet named this masculine figure.

Whatever this masculine referent, he is clearly one who is against Yahweh's purposes and against whom the reader should stand in opposition. Only one character remains with whom the reader can identify. The reader should align with the feminine 'you' who, though once afflicted by Yahweh, is about to experience a positive change in fortunes. Yahweh's ability to effect these promises, as well as to crush his enemies, has already been established: before Yahweh the Divine Warrior the very earth lifts up, 'even the world and all who dwell in it' (1.5).

III. Bounded Meanings?

Reading the book as a whole up to this point seems to settle the ambiguities in 1.11-14, allowing the reader to understand 'he' and 'they' as

Assyrians and to identify with the feminine 'you' who receives good news. But, as in 1.2-10, inconsistencies and tensions remain. The anxiety of reading 1.11-14 is not easily remedied.

That the text would require such a process of reading and rereading, the continual searching for clues, itself precludes any definitive reading. How can one read with any confidence and comfort a text that withholds the answers to so many questions? Is the enemy singular or plural? Masculine or feminine? Is plotting against Yahweh something to be avoided by the Other and/or by the community? What, if like so many good yet dead detectives, the reader has overlooked the barely conspicuous but all-essential clue?

The destabilizing function of Yahweh's admission that 'I afflicted you' (1.12) scarcely can be overestimated. Nahum has to this point in its argument led a reader to see the world as divided into two camps: (1) Nineveh = Yahweh's enemy = one who plots against Yahweh; and (2) you = those who take refuge in him = the one about to be rescued. But the news now delivered alters the equation that Nahum's rhetoric has worked so hard to formulate: 'I afflicted you' suggests that, at least for a time, 'you' were Yahweh's enemy. Was Assyria, then, Yahweh's friend?

Faced with this tension, the reader might retreat to the Isaiah intertexts. Isaiah, after all, affirms that Assyria can be both used and punished by Yahweh in ways that do not compromise his justice. And yet, reading Nahum in light of Isaiah highlights what Nahum is lacking. Unlike Isaiah, Nahum never names Judah's crimes or the censure it might justly face. If Nahum agrees with Isaiah that guilty Judah has been punished by Yahweh by means of Assyrian oppression, where is *Nahum's* judgment against Judah (cf. Isa. 1–2)? Or if, as in Isaiah, Yahweh is now ready to punish the instrument he once used to humble Judah, to what changed conditions is he responding? Judah's repentance (cf. Isa. 37)? Its destruction (cf. Isa. 10.12)?

Perhaps attempting to silence such questions, Nah. 1.12 claims to be divine speech, Yahweh's own words. Yet, such a designation rubs against 1.1's labeling of the entire book of Nahum is a 'book of the vision'. Ironically, the marking of 1.12 as the word of Yahweh unmarks the divine origin of the verses that have preceded it. In turn, the awesome description of the Divine Warrior becomes not Yahweh's self-description but that of the book/author/prophet. Would Yahweh agree to this description of how he treats—and identifies—his friends and his enemies?

Nahum 2*

The dual-sided theme of salvation and punishment that permeates Nahum 1 provides the structure of Nahum 2. After a short announcement of good news to Judah (2.1), the unit turns to a longer, graphic depiction of the siege of Nineveh, told in highly crafted poetic form. Two of the addressees of the book, who have until now been anonymous, are here explicitly named—confirming and yet failing to contain the gap-filling that readers have employed in rendering sense to previous verses.

I. Reading Nahum 2

The announcement of salvation in 2.1, as in the previous unit, is addressed to a feminine singular 'you'. But here, in an appositive, 'you' is explicitly named for the first time: the feminine character with whom the reader has been invited to identify is Judah.

The personification of Judah as female in Nahum is noteworthy yet not unique. Elsewhere in the Hebrew Bible, Judah is always male in non-metaphorical contexts (when the name refers to the son of Jacob and Leah or to the tribe which bears his name). When the term is used to describe the southern kingdom, it usually is paired with masculine verbal forms and masculine pronouns (e.g. Hos. 10.11; 11.12; Isa. 3.8; 11.13), though the feminine also is used (Isa. 7.6; Jer. 3.7-11; 13.19; 14.2; Joel 4.20). The reader's identification with Judah is encouraged he structure of 2.1. The opening particle *hinnēh* arrests the reader's attention (though usually translated 'Look!' or 'Behold!', it is not an imperative but an interjection, perhaps better understood colloquially as 'Hey, you!'). The reader is invited to gaze at the feet of an anonymous bearer of good news, but the commands that follow address Judah. This easy slide from the perspective of the reader to that of Judah aligns their allegiances, inviting a reader to find comfort in the promise to Judah of perpetual relief from the evil who had threatened once before (1.11). Clearly, the 'peace' of the messenger's tidings (2.1) refers not to the bilateral cessation of war but to Judah's victory.

---

*   2.1 in the Hebrew text is 1.15 in many English versions, so that the number of each subsequent verse of ch. 2 in those versions is one less than the corresponding number in the Hebrew texts (e.g. 2.3 in the Hebrew Bible = 2.2 in many English Bibles). The Hebrew verse numbering is used in this commentary.

Like 2.1, Nah. 2.2 addresses a feminine singular 'you', but one whose fate is clearly opposite that of Judah: Judah was called to celebrate (2.1) but this 'you' is invited to mount a defense against an approaching 'scatterer'. In order to reconcile these divergent messages, the reader posits a new addressee, yet unnamed.

This new 'you' is the target of a military siege, the description of which will dramatically build in suspense and intensity in 2.1-11. The advancing enemy is sighted and 'you' are commanded to defend yourself (2.2); parenthetically, Judah is identified as the beneficiary of the destruction (2.3); an army pours through city streets (2.4-6); in a grand climax, the city, finally named as Nineveh, falls (2.7-9); the destruction is surveyed (2.10-11); the ruined city is taunted (2.12-14); and (anti-climatically) Yahweh announces his punishment.

Whose army marches against Nineveh? The mention of a 'scatterer' in Nah. 2.2 provides the first of many clues that the troops belong to Yahweh, the Divine Warrior, since 'scatterer' appears throughout Divine Warrior texts as an epithet for Yahweh (Hab. 3; Zech. 13; Pss. 18; 68; 144; 2 Sam. 22). The cosmic Divine Warrior who marched to vanquish all foes and save all friends in 1.2-10 here fights an earthly battle against a particular enemy.

The battle scene has just begun when it is interrupted by an aside, reminding the reader that the battle about to take place has as its goal the restitution of the 'pride of Jacob', paralleled with 'pride of Israel'. Significantly, the ensuing battle is not for vindicating Judah, who was directly addressed in 2.1 (and implicitly addressed in 1.11-14), but for restoring the honor of Jacob/Israel—the northern kingdom, destroyed by the Assyrians in 721 BCE. Usually in the Hebrew Bible, the attribution of 'pride' to any agent other than Yahweh carries negative connotations; in oracles of judgment, the nations and Judah/Israel are punished for their pride (e.g. 'Lord Yahweh has sworn by himself, says Yahweh, the God of hosts. I abhor the pride of Jacob and hate his strongholds; and I will deliver up the city and all that is in it', Amos 6.8). In Nah. 2.3, however, the sense is one of honor, lost in the shame of the Assyrian destruction of Israel (see, too, Jer. 2.36). This dishonor is described as the 'emptying of emptiers' (the Hebrew noun and verb deriving from the same root, a technique also used in 1.10—'like drunkards drunk').

Having explained why Yahweh marches in battle, the text returns in 2.4 to the battle scene itself. How is the reader to understand the flashing shields and dashing chariots? Are they those of the Assyrian army, frantically but futilely attempting to defend itself against the attack? Such is the reading of 2.4 by some interpreters, who understand the redness of the shields as describing the wealth and polish of the advancing army;

since the battle has not yet begun, the shields cannot be bloody (Roberts 1991: 65; Charles 1989: 189-90). Similarly, most translations consider the 'cypresses' of the verse as military equipment ('spears', KJV, NIV, NASB), though RSV, NRSV, and NASB emend the word to read 'horses'. Several clues, however, support the reading of 2.4-5 as a portrait of Yahweh's divine army. Not only has the epithet 'scatterer' in 2.2 raised this possibility, but also the Divine Warrior poem in Isaiah 63 reveals that Yahweh can begin one battle still stained by the blood of the last. More-over, the MT reading of 'the cypresses are made to reel' in Nah. 2.4 fits well with the description of nature's upheaval upon the Warrior's march: in Nah. 1.4, Lebanon (known for its cypresses) withers, and in Zech. 12.2 the Divine Warrior makes Jerusalem a 'cup of reeling'.

Poetic devices in 2.4-5 heighten the intensity of the scene. The color red, given in parallelism with the rare term 'scarlet', connects the scene with violence and bloodshed (Spronk 1997: 89). The syntax of 2.5 is often disconnected ('chariot', singular; 'race', plural), befitting its con-tent. Like the chariots it describes, phrases flash like lightning, giving the reader glimpses but not the totality of the scene.

The negative connotation of 'stumble' in 2.6 suggests that, yet again, a new unnamed character is being described. 'He' is no longer Yahweh, but the one who directs the defense of the city. Despite his efforts, the city of Nineveh falls in 2.7-9. Compared to the complex syntax and heaped-up phrases of 2.4-6, Nah. 2.7 is terse and direct: in five Hebrew words, the defeat of the enemy that so far has preoccupied the book of Nahum is accomplished.

Most interpreters treat literally the description in 2.7 of the city's fall by the bursting of water gates, based on the much later testimonies of Diodorus Siculus and Xenophon that Nineveh fell by the flooding of its water supply (Charles 1989: 194). Parallels with similar documents, how-ever, suggest that water was a common metaphor for destruction in the ancient Near East. Jeremiah 51 utilizes this image heavily, as do the passages treated in my discussion of Nah. 1.8. In the Sumerian *Lament over the Destruction of Ur*, that city's fall is described as a storm, following Kramer's translation:

> The destructive storm makes the land tremble and quake
> Like the storm of the flood it destroys...the cities.
> The land-annihilating storm set up (its) decrees in the city.
> The all-destroying storm came doing evil... (lines 198-203)

The parallel mention of the 'melting' of the palace further supports the metaphorical nature of 2.7. Similarly, in Nah. 1.5, the hills 'melted' before the Divine Warrior.

Nahum 2.8 has proved problematic for interpreters. The MT reads *huṣṣab gullᵉtâ*. The second verb clearly means '(she) is exiled', but translations of *huṣṣab* range from the name of a princess (KJV) to 'it is determined' (NRSV, NASB, NIV, NKJV). Although Sanderson (1992: 218) identifies 'she' as Ishtar, the city goddess of Nineveh, a more logical identification is Nineveh itself, addressed with a feminine pronoun in 2.2 and soon to be named explicitly as Nineveh in 2.9. Such an understanding of the verse is built into RSV and NAB, who add 'its mistress', and into NIV and NRSV, who add 'the city'. No longer directly addressed, the feminine target of Yahweh's attack is now described in the third person, in a detached, distanced way.

While the use of gender-specific pronouns to describe characters is on some level metaphorical (Nineveh is compared to a woman), the mention of the feminine character's handmaids introduces a new level of metaphorization: the 'she' who is addressed is compared to a particular status of woman, one wealthy enough to possess servants. While the metaphorical description of the woman remains fairly contained in ch. 2, it will burgeon in ch. 3 in the personfication of Nineveh as another distinct type of woman—a prostitute. In Nah. 2.8, the reader hears the rhyming, onomatopoeic sounds of the handmaids' grief, as they moan (*mᵉnahᵃgôt*) and beat their breasts (*mᵉtōppōt*).

In 2.9, without fanfare, the reader receives a crucial piece of information: 'she' is Nineveh, mentioned for the first time since the superscription. This identification of Nineveh with the target of Yahweh's attack has profound implications for the book as a whole. In the unit itself, it serves to contrast two named female characters, Judah and Nineveh—one who can rest from evil (2.1) and one who is now experiencing destruction. In yet another simile ('handmaids moaning like the voice of the dove', 2.8), Nineveh is compared to 'a pool of days', a pool whose water does not last, ephemeral. Commands, shouted to no one in particular (common plural), go unheeded. Yahweh has, indeed, scattered the Assyrians (2.2).

Commands continue into 2.10, in clipped, breathless style. 'Plunder silver! Plunder gold! No end to the amount! Abundance of every precious vessel!' The implied agent of this looting remains obscure. Are the Ninevites told to loot their own city? Is the divine army invited to benefit from the spoils of war? Is this a war about honor (2.3) or about gain (2.10)?

The terseness of style continues into 2.11. Staccato sentences, some without verbs, fire in rapid succession. NRSV well captures the initial alliteration: 'Devastation, desolation, and destruction!' (*bûqâ ûmᵉbûqâ ûmᵉbullāqâ*). Attention then turns to the body's response to terror:

heart melts, knees totter, loins anguish, faces pale (or 'blacken', KJV), despite the call to strength in 2.2.

In the face of a trembling Nineveh, the voice of Nah. 2.12-14 taunts. It steps back from addressing Nineveh directly and asks a rhetorical question about the whereabouts of the lion's den. Four different Hebrew words for lions are used (*'aryēh, gôr/gûr, lābî', kᵉpîr*), translated in the NRSV with five (*gûr* translated as 'cub' in 2.12 [Eng. 2.11] and as ' whelp' in 2.13 [Eng. 2.12]). Attempts to assign each character a role in the royal family are forced, but the focus of the passage is clearly on the male lion's role of protection and provision. The lion, who has provided spoil for the cubs and for the lioness (2.13), is nowhere to be found (2.12).

As the climax of the unit, 2.14 both clarifies and obscures. On the one hand, it assigns roles in the leonine imagery: 'you' (feminine, i.e., Nineveh) are the one whose young lions will be eaten by the sword, a particularly ironic fate for a nation well known for its association with the lion. Yahweh is the one who will take away the spoil (from the same root as NRSV 'tore' in 2.13). On the other hand, the specific gender roles attributed to the domestic scene in the lion's den raise the possibility that Nineveh might be the lioness, the one who is described as provided for by another.

That the fate of Nineveh is opposite that to of Judah is expressed poetically by the ending of 2.14. Nahum 2.1 opened with a messenger bringing good news to Judah, and 2.14 ends with the obliteration of Assyria's messengers. The one responsible for both of their fates is Yahweh, the Divine Warrior.

Or is the humiliation of Nineveh to take place in the future? The variation in the verb tenses throughout the unit does not made clear the temporality of the event. In 2.2-3, the verbs are perfect (completed action)—Yahweh has already acted. In 2.4-6, imperfects and participles predominate—Nineveh's destruction is in progress. In 2.7-8, perfects return—Nineveh has fallen. In 2.9-11, most phrases lack verbs, though a few participles and one perfect appear—Nineveh is again shown in the process of falling. In 2.14, verbs are again imperfect. Should the verbs be understood as describing the future fate of the city? Or are these imperfects, like the previous ones, describing the current work Yahweh is doing? Is the reader to imagine that the fall of Nineveh is now or later? And if later, when?

Read as an isolated unit, Nahum 2 confronts the reader with a strong contrast between the fates of Judah and Nineveh, both described as feminine. Judah is called to rejoice because her oppression has ended; Nineveh is described as under siege by Yahweh, the Divine Warrior. The fate of the latter is described in greater detail than that of the former.

The reader sees, smells, and hears the siege of Nineveh but is given no taste of Judah's feasts.

II. Reading Nahum 2 with Nahum 1

When read in conjunction with Nahum 1, the present unit spawns additional reading consequences. Nahum 2 extends backward for the reader, confirming and altering perceptions formed by a reading of Nah. 1.1-14. The reading encounter with Nahum 1 also pushes forward, shaping an understanding of Nahum 2.

As I discussed above, Nahum 1 plagued the reader with multiple identity crises: the frequent use of pronouns forced readers to search for clues (especially within the superscription) by which to name 'you' and 'they'. On one level, Nah. 2.1-14 soothes identity anxiety by naming two addressees. Although Nineveh went unmentioned from 1.2 to 2.8, its explicit naming in 2.9 clarifies that the target of the vengeful and angry Yahweh of the theophany in 1.2-8 is the foreign city; she is the 'adversary' and 'enemy' of Yahweh (1.8), and whoever receives the threat of 1.14 must be related to her. The explicit naming of Nineveh in 2.9 ties the book to its superscription: this book is indeed a *maśśā'* against Nineveh, heaping judgment on the Other.

By announcing to Judah the time for celebration, 2.1 explicitly names the beneficiary of Yahweh's favor. Judah is the 'one who takes refuge', the one for whom Yahweh's vengeance is 'good' (1.7), the one who will be 'afflicted no more' (1.12). The mention of Judah's good fortune confirms that Nahum is a *maśśā'*, a book in which the fate of 'us' is a mirror image of the fate of 'them'. Invited through syntax to identify not with Nineveh but with Judah, the reader need not fear the wrath of the Divine Warrior: Yahweh takes vengeance on Nineveh ('his enemies', 1.2) and protects Judah ('those who take refuge in him', 1.7).

When Nahum 2 is read in conjunction with the Divine Warrior hymn in Nahum 1, the book's portrait of Nineveh takes on new dimensions. The one who threatened Judah is linked with the enemy against whom Yahweh marches: Judah's enemies are equated with Yahweh's enemies. In addition, the historically concrete Nineveh takes on a cosmic character. Nineveh is not just a threat to Judah but is linked with the chaos that provokes Yahweh's theophany in Nahum 1. Rather than becoming a symbol for evil in the book of Nahum, Nineveh's evil is magnified to cosmic dimensions. With such a strong image of the divine army in place, the reader is encouraged to identify the army described in Nahum 2 as that of Yahweh, not of the Assyrians.

III. Lingering Questions

While the portrait of the fall of Nineveh in 2.1-14 gives the book of
Nahum a concrete focus and identifies some of its primary characters, it
also leaves readers with troubling questions.

A. Naming Names

By identifying Yahweh's friend as Judah (2.1) and Yahweh's enemy as
Nineveh, Nahum 2 attempts to soothe the anxiety that is provoked by
reading Nahum 1; the reader, uncertain whether to identify with the
enemy of Yahweh (1.2, 8) or with Yahweh's friend (1.7, 12), is assured
that Yahweh's raging march is against Nineveh alone. But fear is not
easily forgotten, even in times of safety. The experience of reading
Nahum 1 and the questions that it engenders are not erased by the
simple declarations of Nahum 2.

The fact that Nahum 2 continues to obscure identities feeds the very
reading anxieties it aims to squelch. Why do I need to search for clues to
know whose armies are described in 2.4-5? If the distinction between
Yahweh and the enemy is so stark, then why can I not be sure which this
is? And why do I still not know the identity of the masculine 'you' in 1.14
and the male lion in 2.1? Both chapters have ended with promises of *his*
destruction, and I still do not know who *he* is.

B. Gender

The unnamed, lingering male who ends both ch. 1 and ch. 2 also raises
questions about the very schema in which Nahum is presenting its
message. In the first two chapters, the book has staked a clear (if uneasy)
dichotomy between 'us' and 'them'—one deserving Yahweh's comfort
and the other his wrath. In the explicit naming of Judah and Nineveh in
ch. 2, both 'we' and 'they' are feminine. A quite different distinction was
made in 1.11-14, where the contrast was between the positive feminine
character and the negative male character. In ch. 1, the reader was encouraged to identify with the female against the male; now in ch. 2, the
reader is encouraged to identify with the good woman over against the
bad woman. In ch. 2 males are officers and soldiers, but not persons
with whom to identify.

The female vs female contrast in ch. 2 interacts strangely with the lion
imagery of 2.12-13. Here (differently from nature) the male lion is the
one who provides for the female and the cubs. This assignment of
responsibility, ironically, absolves Nineveh herself; her fall is due to the
failure of the male who was to protect her. Despite the apparently
female focus of this chapter, is the issue really one between males?

Yahweh will protect his woman, Judah. But who has failed to protect Nineveh?

C. Shame

The underlying issues of maleness also surface in 2.3. While the verse is parenthetical in the structure of 2.2-13, it is nonetheless basic to the chapter's ideology: the defeat (and, later in ch. 3, the humiliation) of Nineveh functions to restore honor. Significantly, however, the offended pride is not that of Judah (feminine) but of Jacob/Israel (masculine). The exaltation of one female (Judah) and the humiliation of another (Nineveh) will restore honor to a male (Jacob/Israel).

Whose is the male honor that has been threatened? A nation long ago destroyed? Or perhaps another male figure who, like the lion (2.11-12), failed to protect his woman, despite his claims that he chose not to do so (1.12)?

D. Pleasure

Nahum 2.2-13 is powerful poetry. The facetious imperatives addressed to the doomed Assyrian soldiers; the vivid colors of the advancing army's uniforms; the variety of verbs describing the movement of the horses; the comparison of the women of the city to mourning doves and the city to receding water; the alliteration of language; the use of similes and onomatopoeia; the ironic use of Assyrian lion imagery; and the rhetorical, mocking questions thrown at the unnamed male—all these allow a reader to envision the scene, to imagine a city in the process of being destroyed.

These literary features also produce pleasure. The sounds of the Other's terror are made appealing to the ear, to the senses. Built in to the very craft of the book is delight in—or at least fascination with—another's suffering. Or perhaps, as I will explore in 'Nahum and Atrocity', the effect of such pleasure is to destabilize reading.

Nahum 3

This unit parallels Nahum 2 in several ways. *Thematically*, Nahum 3 repeats many of the motifs of Nahum 2—also personifying Nineveh as a woman and offering yet another glimpse of Nineveh's fall. *Stylistically*, the chapter uses many of the poetic features employed in ch. 2—simile, personification, direct address, verbless sentences, and assonance and alliteration. *Structurally*, both chapters follow similar patterns—each begins with a description of the city's siege; stops to describe Nineveh in metaphorical terms; returns to the images of the siege; compares the Assyrians to animals; and ends with an announcement of disaster.

In its recapitulation, however, ch. 3 intensifies all the elements of ch. 2. Nineveh is imagined not just as a woman but as a prostitute; her punishment is not just exile but the sexual humiliation of a whore. Scenes of the battle are more graphic, and the victims less stylized. Chapter 3 also divulges a piece of information that is vital to understanding the book of Nahum. In the penultimate verse, Nahum identifies the male character that has gone unnamed throughout the book.

I. Reading Nahum 3

A. 3.1-3

Nahum 3.1 opens with an interjection of grief: *hôy*, 'Woe' (NRSV, 'Ah'). As an interjection, its implied speaker is the book's implied author (the prophet and/or God), a perspective that the reader has been trained to honor from the beginning of the book. This command for the reader to grieve is then immediately subverted, shown to be sarcastic, as the one to be mourned is not a sympathetic figure but a 'city of blood/blood-shed, full of lies'. This city is filled with plunder and with prey, just as the lion's den was in 2.13, a repetition which effectively equates the 'city of blood' with the one who was taunted in 2.12-13 and subsequently identified as Nineveh in 2.8. The connection of 3.1 with 2.12-13 further invites the reader to understand the prey and plunder as those captured by Nineveh in its raids of others, although, syntactically, 'prey and plunder' could equally well refer to the riches that a sack of Nineveh offers to any invading army.

Nahum 3.2-3 rehearses much of 2.5-11, though in greater detail and with more gore. As in ch. 2, nouns are strung together without verbs, giving not a narrative but isolated sensations of a city being destroyed.

The NRSV's use of exclamation marks and its choice of strong verbs (e.g. the 'crack' of the whip vs KJV's 'noise') captures well the feel of the Hebrew. As before, we *see* images of the chariots' motion (in 2.5, they dart like lightning; in 3.2, they skip about), the flashing of spear and sword, but we now also *hear* sounds of the whip and of the rumbling wheel.

Thrown into the mass of phrases is the acknowledgment of a reality that ch. 2 attempted to obscure: in the siege of Nineveh, people die. The earlier description of the city's fall in 2.7-8 used metaphor and simile to describe the city's fall. Her handmaids were led away 'like' doves, and Nineveh was 'like' a pool; and even 2.11, which described emotional terror, never mentioned *whose* heart melts, *whose* knees totter, and *whose* loins anguish (*sic*). In contrast, Nah. 3.3 adds human corpses to the battle scene, mentioning them four times, and offering one of the most haunting phrases in the book: 'piles of dead, heaps of corpses, dead bodies without end—they stumble over the bodies!' (NRSV).

And yet, even in this recognition that people die, ch. 3 goes no further than ch. 2 in humanizing the dead or in identifying the victors. *Who* dies in Nineveh? Men? Women? Children? *How* do they die? Quickly? Slowly? *Whose* horse lifts up? Are 'they' who stumble over the bodies to be understood as the Assyrian officers who stumbled in 2.6? Or are 'they' the army of Yahweh the Warrior, stepping over the mass of dead?

B. 3.4-7

This section expands and elaborates on the image of the city as a woman that began in Nahum 2. Here, in gender-specific derogatory language, Nineveh is called *zônâ*—a prostitute.

The term *zônâ* carries multiple nuances in the Hebrew Bible. Literally, it refers to a professional prostitute, one who receives money for sexual acts. The term describes the activities of Tamar (Gen. 38) and Rahab (Josh. 2), and its prohibition is paralleled with that of a male prostitute in Deut. 23.18. Figuratively, however, *zônâ* refers to any promiscuous woman. In Deut. 22.21, for example, a young woman found not to be a virgin is called a *zônâ* and Ezek. 23.3 uses the term to accuse young women of promiscuous behavior.

Its figurative sense of 'promiscuity' extends further to describe religious unfaithfulness. In the Pentateuch, the Deuteronomistic History, and occasionally in Psalms, verbal forms of *zônâ* describe the worship of deities other than Yahweh (Exod. 34.15-16; Lev. 20.5-6; Deut. 31.16; Josh. 2.1; Judg. 2, 8; Pss. 73; 106). In the prophetic literature, *zônâ* is used frequently in the marriage metaphor, in which God's relation to Israel and/or Judah is compared to a man's relation to his wife and in which religious unfaithfulness is compared to adultery. In Isa. 57.3, Jer. 3.8, and Hos. 4.13-14 the roots *nā'ap* ('commit adultery') and *zānâ* stand in synonymous parallelism, and in the lengthy expositions of the metaphor in Hosea 2 and Ezekiel 16 and 23 both charges are made against unfaithful women.

Such usages suggest that *zônâ* refers to any woman who does not meet societal expectations of sexual conduct. Most often it is a slur which demeans by equating the object of scorn with women who sell their sexual services. Hence, while some interpreters have attempted to specify Nineveh's acts of promiscuity, identifying them as her treaties with multiple partners, the reference may be a slur more than an analogy. Nahum, having inherited the tradition of personifying cities as women, uses the culture's definition of the worst kind of woman, the whore, as a slur by which to demean Nineveh.

While, by analogy, *zônà* can be used for the activity of males (Israel and/or Judah and their male inhabitants can be accused of being [like] a *zônâ*), the slur is distinctively female in orientation. It relies on the internal logic of patriarchy—the appropriateness of expressions of female sexuality is determined by the rights of men: a woman's sexuality is 'owned' by her father until transferred to her husband. Within patriarchy, the professional prostitute remains in a liminal position. Her sexuality owned by no male, her actions do not violate male property rights, and yet her perpetual promiscuity threatens the values that undergird patriarchy's expectations for women. According to Bird (1989: 79), 'the prostitute is that "other woman", tolerated but stigmatized, desired but ostracized'.

By calling Nineveh *zônâ*, Nahum sets Nineveh as the ultimate Other. The city is not only female and foreign, but also a woman on the boundaries of society. Nahum 3.4 confirms her dual status. She is described as appealing, 'gracefully alluring', but the identification of the one who finds her attractive is never addressed; rather than the attraction to her being owned by someone (by the implied author or by Yahweh), it is attributed to her own sorcery. As in 2 Kgs 9.22 and Isa. 57.3, the charge of *zônâ* is paired with that of witchcraft.

The insistence that punishment must fit the crime runs throughout the book of Nahum, as well as the Hebrew Bible. The idea is built into the vocabulary of this section: for the multitude (*rōb*) of Nineveh's harlotries (3.4), there are multitudes (*rōb*) of slain (3.3). Similarly, just as the demeaning of Nineveh was described in explicit sexual terms, so too is Nineveh's punishment.

The punishment that awaits the promiscuous Nineveh is outlined in 3.5-7. The first verb in 3.5 is usually translated as the 'uncovering' of the skirt, although the verbal root *gālâ* is the same one in 2.8, translated in the NRSV as 'exile'. The exposure of a woman's genitalia as a means of humiliation is well known from the prophetic literature, as in Isa. 47.2-3 where daughter Babylon is stripped and humiliated and in Hos. 2.2-3 where stripping is preliminary to the death of the woman. 'Uncovering' often also carries the sense of sexual violation: in Lev. 8.18, it is paralleled with taking a woman as rival to her sister; in the description of Israel's whoring in Ezek. 16.36, it is paralleled with the outpouring of lust, and in Jer. 13.22 Judah is not only exposed but also 'violated'.

Nahum 3.5 is marked as divine speech, only the third such indication in the book. Here, Yahweh not only announces the prostitute's punishment but also decrees that he will carry it out himself. *He* will do the uncovering; *he* will throw filth on her and despise her; *he* will make others look upon her. Indeed, 3.5-7 expresses great concern about the gaze of others. Not only will nations and kingdoms see Nineveh's shame (3.5), but she will also be a 'sight' (3.6) and all will recoil from seeing her (3.7).

In this section, Yahweh is characterized as a man who sexually assaults Nineveh in return for her promiscuity, as other nations, characterized as men, gaze at her nakedness. Nineveh becomes a 'spectacle'—something to observe. This motif of a woman, described as both attractive and as a whore, being sexually assaulted while others watch, is one frequent in pornographic literature, leading some feminist scholars to designate these biblical passages 'pornoprophetics'.

Differently from most prophetic literature, however, Nahum directs the punishment of one called a whore against a nation other than Israel or Judah. Uniquely here, Yahweh punishes the promiscuity of one with whom he is not in covenant/marriage relationship. Though in Isaiah 23 Tyre receives both Yahweh's punishment and the label of *zônâ*, Tyre is not punished *for* promiscuity; rather, the proceeds of her activities are dedicated to Yahweh (Isa. 23.18).

After such a scathing and violent description of Nineveh's pending fate, the rhetorical questions of those who see the devastated Nineveh are highly ironic. Who will grieve her? Not the implied author who began the chapter with a call to the reader of 'Woe!' From where will she receive comforters (verbal root *nāḥam*)? Not from Nahum, the character who author-izes this book.

C. 3.8-13

This section taunts Nineveh, asking her to compare herself to another feminized city, No-Amon (Thebes), a well-defended Egyptian city conquered by the Assyrian king Ashurbanipal in 663 BCE. Despite her extensive defenses and numerous allies (Cush, Put, the Libyans), Thebes fell.

Since what happened to Thebes will happen to Nineveh, the description of Thebes' woes serves as a series of threats against Nahum's own foe. If *Thebes* went into exile/was uncovered (*gālâ*, also 2.8, 3.5), if *her* children were dashed to pieces, then Nineveh can expect the same treatment. Such a rhetorical device (threatening Nineveh by describing the fate of Thebes) allows Nahum's author to insinuate, without announcing outright, that Ninevite children will be killed. The identities of the child-killers remains nameless: the passive verb 'were dashed to pieces' in 3.10 does not indicate who killed the Theban children, or, in the comparison, who will kill the Ninevite children. The verbs that follow also avoid naming the agent(s) of destruction: 'they' cast lots for her nobles and her honored citizens 'were bound'.

The 'also, too' of 3.11 suggests that the punishments now announced on Nineveh were shared by Thebes. Both became drunk, an image frequently used in the prophets for the effect of punishment (Jer. 13.13; 25.15-29; 48.26; 49.12; 51.7, 39; Obad. 16; Hab. 2.15-16; Zech. 12.2; Lam. 4.21; Ezek. 23.31-34). The second punishment, 'you will become concealed' (NAS, KJV, NKJV: 'you shall be hidden') provides a strong parallel with 'seeking refuge' which follows, but its relation to the earlier threat of Nineveh's uncovering (3.5) is intriguing. Are these punishments in tension with one another, or will Nineveh seek cover after her stripping by Yahweh? If this was Thebes' fate as well, was she also stripped? By whom?

Nahum 3.12 and 3.13 both describe the vulnerability of Nineveh, but while 3.12 clearly utilizes simile (the city is as ready to fall as ripe figs), the nature of 3.13 is more contested. Magdalene (1995: 333), for example, understands 3.13a as demeaning Assyrian warriors by comparing them to (weak) women, a reading which she supports by highlighting the double-entendre of the rest of the verse: if 'gates' is translated as 'vagina', as in Isa. 3.26, the verse threatens the feminized Assyrian soldiers with the horror of sexual violation. Taking an opposite view, Floyd (2000: 74) reads the verse not as metaphorical but as a literal indication that the death of warriors has left only women in the city. Both of these readings—the metaphorical and the literal—work in 3.13, primarily because of the transitional nature of the verse in the unit. In its literary function, 3.12 bridges the metaphorical comparisons of 3.8-12 and the concrete description of the siege of the city that follows in 3.14-15.

D. 3.14-19

After Nineveh has been compared to Thebes, a city known to have fallen, the encouragement of the Assyrians to defend themselves in 3.14 can only be facetious. Indeed, 3.15 makes clear that the Assyrians will perish at the very site of their own attempts at self-defense: *there* the fire will devour (as in 3.13); and the war sword will devour as the locust devours.

While 3.15b highlights the legendary appetite of locusts for the purposes of comparison, the verses that follow draw upon others of their characteristics, utilizing extended locust-related vocabulary (three different Hebrew words are used to describe these devourers). In 3.15c-16a, the huge numbers in which locusts congregate suggest a ready hyperbole: even if the Assyrians multiply like locusts, they have no chance of escape. In 3.16c-17, the rapid arrivals and departures of locusts provide a simile for the cowardly retreat of Assyrian officials: guards and scribes fly away like locusts, leaving the city unprotected.

In the midst of this extensive locust imagery, the charge in 3.16 that Nineveh has multiplied its merchants stands out, offering several possibilities for interpretation. On the one hand, the verse may be a rare concrete naming of Nineveh's crimes. Up to this point in the book, the accusations against Nineveh have been metaphorical or generic: she is punished 'because Yahweh is restoring the majesty of Jacob' (2.3) and 'because of the countless whorings of the whore' (3.4). If 3.16a is understood as accusatory, then Nineveh's control over international trade is given as one of its crimes. On the other hand, the half-verse may be descriptive, a further example of those within Assyria whose loyalty is ephemeral; just like the guards and the scribes, the Assyrian merchants, numerous as the stars, abandon the people as quickly as a locust sheds its skin and flies away.

In naming merchants, guards, and scribes, Nah. 3.17 comes closer than the book has up to this point to naming real people in Assyria. In 3.17, personified Nineveh is still addressed, but real persons begin to get the blame. Merchants, guards, and scribes are compared to locusts who disappear when things heat up.

The first intimations, offered in 3.16-17, that not everyone in Nineveh bears equal responsibility for cruelty find full affirmation in 3.18-19. The addressee changes abruptly: 'you' is now masculine singular, and, in an appositive, the male character that has remained obscure throughout the book is finally named: 'he' is the king of Assyria. In these verses, faults are no longer those of Nineveh and all its inhabitants; rather, the people are scattered (innocent) sheep because their leaders sleep. The king, not Nineveh, receives the final threats. There is no healing of his wound, just as there was no comfort for Nineveh in 3.7. Everyone rejoices because everyone has felt his cruelty.

II. Reading Nahum 3 in Light of Nahum 1–2

The three anonymous addressees of Nahum 1–2 have been named pro-
gressively in the course of the book. The comforted feminine character,
addressed as 'you' in 1.11-14, was identified as Judah in 2.1. The
threatened feminine character, addressed as 'you' in 2.2 and as 'she' in
2.8, was identified as Nineveh in 2.9. The threatened male character (the
referent of 'his' in 1.13, addressed as 'you' in 1.14, and implied in the
leonine analogy in 2.13) is only named as the king of Assyria in the
penultimate verse of the book.

By identifying the male object of threat as the king of Assyria, Nahum 3
answers some of the reading queries raised by earlier parts of the book.
His is the only name provided for the generic male references: *he*
becomes equated with the enemy of Yahweh (1.2); *his* is the rod that
will be broken (1.13); *his* is the grave that will be set (1.14); and *he* is the
lion who is no longer able to protect his den (2.12-14).

Thus linked with earlier passages, the king of Assyria assumes greater
culpability than the last two verses would suggest if they are read alone.
Nineveh no longer stands as the primary guilty party. Indeed, once the
king of Assyria is identified with the lion of the analogy in 2.12-14—the
one who tears prey, filling his dens with torn flesh—Nineveh becomes
the victim, the one whose male could not protect her. Yahweh protects
Judah, but the king of Assyria cannot protect Nineveh.

Similarly, calling the leaders of Assyria 'shepherds' functions in multi-
form ways. It piles up metaphors that clash with one another: the King-
as-lion, an image produced when the king is named as the male addressee of the book, is said ironically to oversee shepherds; the one who is
described as the predator in 2.12 is mocked in 3.18 for having shepherds
who slumber; the one whose people are described in 3.19 as scattered
sheep is depicted in 2.12 as bringing strangled prey into the den.

The attention that Nahum ultimately gives to the king of Assyria leaves
the reader with questions. Whose crimes warrant Yahweh's punishment?
The king's? Nineveh's? The entire population of Assyria? Who, exactly, is
God's enemy, the one against whom the Divine Warrior marches?

III. Lingering Issues

The extended female personification of Nineveh in Nahum 3, particularly
its sexualized language, has implications for the book as a whole. As
I have argued above, the accusation of 'whore' is a slur, a charge of
promiscuity less than an allegorical treatment of Assyria's many partners.
Nonetheless, fundamental to the concept of *zônâ* is the absence of a
male to legitimate sexual activity.

Bird (1989: 80), in her classic study of the 'harlot' in Hebrew Bible texts, argues to the contrary: 'Although the underlying metaphor is that of marriage, the use of *zānâ* rather than *nā'ap* serves to emphasize promiscuity rather than infidelity, "wantonness" rather than violation of marriage contract or covenant.' The first part of her statement, however, suggests that marriage remains the ideological backdrop against which *zônâ* stands out, as does her explanation that *znh* is not used for incest or other prohibited relationships, such as homosexual relations or bestiality. It focuses on the absence of a marriage bond *between otherwise acceptable partners* (1989: 90 n. 13; italics mine). That is, what makes a whore a whore is the absence of a husband.

The marital dimensions of *zônâ* are further highlighted in an intertextual reading of Nahum with other prophetic books. As we have seen above, in the prevalent marriage metaphor of the prophets, the charges of prostitution and adultery are often paired (Jer. 3.8, where adultery and prostitution are treated as synonyms; also Hos. 4.13-14; Isa. 1.21), and the kind of punishment that Nineveh receives is that which the adulterous wife receives in Hosea and Ezekiel.

Nahum's use of *zônâ* raises the issue of marriage and of legitimate partnership, even if inadvertently. Which males have been dishonored by Nineveh's promiscuity? While in prophetic marriage metaphor Yahweh's own honor is at stake, Yahweh's interest in Nineveh's promiscuity is not so clear.

Perhaps, when considered in light of the book's ending, Yahweh's interest is not really with Nineveh at all, but rather with her male—the king of Assyria. Is the sexual assault (rape?) of Nineveh a way to shame her male, a dynamic known all too well from contemporary accounts of war? Does the repetitive concern in 3.5-7 with those who will gaze at Nineveh's shame suggest that it is for the sake of others, and not for the crimes of Nineveh herself, that she is sexually assaulted?

When read this way, the book of Nahum speaks of a struggle between two males—Yahweh and the king of Assyria—fought on the bodies of their women (Judah and Nineveh). Just as Nineveh was pitted against Thebes, so too Nineveh and Judah are pitted against each other for the sake of others' concerns. The supposedly parenthetical comment in 2.3 takes on new meaning in light of these observations: the good news proclaimed by the messenger is less about the comfort of Judah herself than the restoration of the honor of Jacob and Israel.

Perhaps even more destabilizing to the book is the recognition in Nahum's final verses that not all Assyrians are the same. By blaming merchants, princes, and scribes for their desertion and by comparing the leaders of Assyria to faithless shepherds—suggesting that average

Assyrians are themselves victims—the close of Nahum undercuts its beginning. If there are different levels of blame and if the enemy is also a victim, then the distinction between the friend and the enemy loses its razor-sharp edge. If this is not ultimately a *maśśā'* against Nineveh, then what am I to expect from a Divine Warrior God whose intent is that of revenge for wrong?

Plate 1. Layard in Assyria. (The transferral of Assyrian remains to Britain bolstered British prestige. Notice the relative positions and activities of the 'natives' vs the British overseers. Frontispiece to Austen Henry Layard, *Nineveh and its Remains* [New York: George P. Putnam, 1849]. Public domain copyright.)

Plate 2. Assyria and the Lion. (Throughout Assyrian art, the lion is associated with Assyrian might, making the lion's den allegory in Nah. 2.12-14 particularly insulting. Here, a lion leaps at Ashurnasirpal's chariot. From Nimrud. British Museum. Detail of WA 124534 [©Copyright The British Museum].)

Plate 3. Fall of Lachish (1). (Reliefs like this one extolling Sennacherib's conquest of Lachish advertised Assyrian success in war. British Museum. WA 124908-10 [©Copyright The British Museum].)

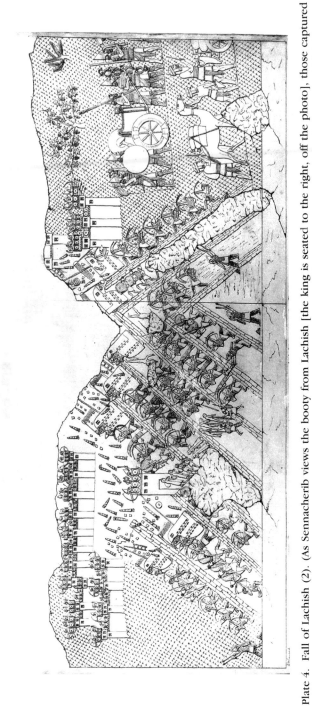

Plate 4. Fall of Lachish (2). (As Sennacherib views the booty from Lachish [the king is seated to the right, off the photo], those captured hang on stakes [third register to the left of centre] and women are carted off [fifth register to the left of centre]. British Museum. WA 124905-7 [©Copyright The British Museum].)

Plate 5. Detail from the Battle of Til-Tuba. (This battle scene not only depicts the violence of Assyrian warfare but also the aesthetic play that Bersani and Dutoit describe. Note the clashing lines of the two horses at right and the complex interplay of their legs. British Museum. Detail of WA 124801 [©Copyright The British Museum].)

Plate 6. 'Heaps of bodies...' (Nah. 3.3). (American soldiers walk past rows of corpses removed from the barracks on their left. Dora-Mittel-bau. Photo credit: Donald S. Robinson, courtesy of United States Holocaust Memorial Museum archives.)

Plate 7. '...piles of corpses...' (Nah. 3.3). (Bodies of prisoners killed in the Nordhausen concentration camp. Photo credit: Michael Mumma, courtesy of United States Holocaust Memorial Museum archives.)

Plate 8. 'I will…make you a spectacle…' (Nah. 3.6). (A group of German soldiers and civilians look on as a Jewish man is forced to cut the beard of another in Tomaszow Mazowiecki. Photo credit: Main Commission for the Prosecution of the Crimes against the Polish Nation, courtesy of United States Holocaust Memorial Museum archives.)

Plate 9. 'Even her infants were dashed in pieces...' (Naḥ. 3.10). (Child survivors of Auschwitz. Photo credit: Belarussian State Archive of Documentary Film and Photography, courtesy of United States Holocaust Memorial Museum archives.)

Plate 10. Children and War. (Faces attempt to personalize the mass graves at Cana, Lebanon, after the 1995 bombing. Photo credit: Ann Webber.)

Plate 11. Children and Global Conflict. (Children at the Gaza refugee camp. Photo by author.)

Plate 12. The Pathos of the Lioness. (This famous Assyrian relief shows the pathos of the dying lioness, without denying her ferocious nature. British Museum. WA 124856 [©Copyright The British Museum].)

Nahum and (Wo)men

As I have traced throughout the commentary, gender plays an important role in the rhetoric of the book of Nahum. The personification of Nineveh, Judah, and Thebes as females, as well as the enigmatic masculine and feminine pronouns whose progressive identification grant suspense and texture to the book, depend on (and construct) notions of gender identity and differentiation in order to communicate.

In this chapter, I further explore gender construction and gender ideology in Nahum. First, I evaluate previous feminist responses to Nahum and then turn to my own contribution.

I. Putting Women on Top

A. Feminist Resistance to the Marriage Metaphor

Feminist responses to Nahum have tended to focus on the treatment of Nineveh in ch. 3. Called a whore, Nineveh is sexually humiliated or raped as punishment for her 'countless debaucheries', as others are called to watch.

This scene is usually treated as a variation on the theme of violence against women that runs throughout the prophetic corpus. In Hosea, Isaiah, Jeremiah, Ezekiel, and elsewhere in the prophets, the nation and/or the city is personified as a female who has been unfaithful to her husband: in this classic 'marriage metaphor', God's impending destruction of the nation is compared to a husband's physical punishment of his wife for her sexual infidelity. Throughout these texts, the punishment of the wife is related in painstaking detail and sexually explicit vocabulary.

This metaphor poses multiple complications for women readers. Cheryl Exum (1995: 249-50) explains the complexity of identification:

> Female readers are placed in a double bind: on the one hand we are asked to sympathize with God and identify with his point of view. To the extent we do so, we read these texts against our own interests. On the other hand, by definition we are identified with the object that elicits scorn and abuse. This involves acceptance if not of guilt, then at least of the indictment of our sex that these texts represent.

Because it relegates woman to an object of abusive sexual fantasy, many feminists have dubbed this material 'pornoprophetic'—a label chosen to underscore the male perspective of the metaphor, as well as the danger that it holds for women and girls.

Feminist resistance to the metaphor has followed two primary paths: (1) the exposure and naming of the patriarchal assumptions on which it depends; and (2) the assumption of a position of advocacy for the woman in the text. Feminist interpreters refuse to identify with God, the 'hero' of the metaphor, and read instead with the victim. In so doing, feminists read against the perspective of the narrator; they 'counter-read'. (For an example of this kind of reading, see Pardes 1992.)

B. Feminists on Nahum

1. *Judith Sanderson*. To date, no monograph-length treatment of Nahum reads from a feminist perspective. Judith Sanderson's entry in *The Women's Bible Commentary* remains the only feminist discussion focused on Nahum. Indeed, given that most feminist treatments of prophetic materials have concentrated on Hosea, Jeremiah, and Ezekiel (which use extended feminine personification), *The Women's Bible Commentary* addresses this imbalance by offering women's comments on all biblical books.

After a brief overview of the historical context of Nahum, Sanderson focuses on the violence against Woman Nineveh in Nahum 3, traversing in fairly equal measure the paths of explanation and advocacy. In her explanatory mode, Sanderson outlines the ambivalent role of the prostitute in ancient Israel: while prostitution was legal in the ancient world, it remained a threat to patriarchal control of women's sexuality. In her resisting mode, Sanderson stresses Nahum's particular offense of attributing the rape of Nineveh to Yahweh himself and calls for contemporary readers to refuse to perpetuate such an image of God:

> What would it mean to worship a God who is portrayed as raping women when angry?... To involve God in an image of sexual violence is, in a profound way, somehow to justify it and thereby to sanction it for human males who are for any reason angry with a woman (1992: 221).

> No aspect of God's relationship with humankind can be represented in the modern world by an image that depends on a destructive view of women's bodied selves (1992: 220).

Sanderson acknowledges that Assyrian brutality gave rise to the intense anger expressed in the book of Nahum but maintains that modern readers must resist the continued use of the misogynist metaphor in which it is couched.

While Sanderson's is the only study solely devoted to feminist concern with Nahum, numerous other critics deal with Nahum in the context of the general issue of violence against women in the prophetic books. I consider here a representative sample of how feminists have responded to Nahum.

2. *Rachel Magdalene.* Magdalene's study of the language of divine sexual abuse devotes most of its attention to explaining the ancient context of the relevant material. In discussing Nahum, she argues that the book's language reflects not the prophetic marriage metaphor but rather the curse formulae of ancient Near Eastern treaty documents. Within Delbert Hillers's (1964) compilation of curses against a vassal who breaks a treaty, she discerns three that bear strong similarity with Nahum 3: (1) his city will become a prostitute; (2) his city will be stripped like a prostitute; and (3) his wives will be raped.

The connection of this latter curse with Nahum 3 is clearest, Magdalene argues, when the sexual connotations of 2.7-8 and 3.13 are appreciated. In other prophetic texts such as Isa. 3.17 and 26, *pōt* ('opening' or 'vagina') is a wordplay on *petaḥ*, 'gate'. While Magdalene does not clarify that Nahum uses a different noun for 'gate' (*šaʿar*, 3.13) and that *petaḥ* appears in verbal form ('are opened'), she does argue persuasively for sexual innuendo in Nahum.

Explaining the ancient logic of the metaphor, Magdalene (1995: 347) suggests that, in a world in which such curses were well known and understood as 'fair', the rape of Nineveh is a just punishment:

> Given the nature of ancient Near Eastern treaties and their curses, the public sexual humiliation or rape of the underling's cities/women is an appropriate response to any perceived or actual violations of existing agreements between God and his people.

Like Sanderson, however, Magdalene (1995: 352) maintains that the *continued* use of these images of violence against women is an ethical problem—'We must stand against the use of such texts as religious metaphor.' The majority of her article, however, is devoted to explaining the ancient mind-set that underlies images of divine sexual abuse.

3. *Susan Thistlethwaite.* In her consideration of rape and war in the Hebrew Bible, Thistlethwaite (1993) joins Sanderson and Magdalene in explaining the patriarchal logic that views the rape of women as the humiliation of the men to whom they 'belong': in a culture dedicated to patrilineal descent and the legitimacy of sons, women's sexuality is an instrument through which social control is maintained. The majority of Thistlethwaite's article, however, focuses on the vast differences between the ancient and contemporary worlds. In terms of rape, the Bible does not deem sexual violence in war as rape and only regulates such activity when it impinges on the legitimacy of children. In terms of war, the highly technological, secular character of modern battle contrasts sharply with ancient hand-to-hand combat that was considered to be led by

deities. These disjunctions, Thistlethwaite argues, not only render 'rape' as a metaphor for war obsolete but also call for new, more powerful metaphors to galvanize resistence to war.

4. *Pamela Gordon and Harold C. Washington*. Gordon and Washington, like the commentators previously discussed, point to patriarchy as the necessary logic underlying the description of Nineveh's humiliation in Nahum 3:

> Thus the social base of the biblical metaphor of city as woman is the patriarchal household, with its ever present threat of violence as a sanction for the control of women... The intrinsic violence of the city-as-woman metaphor is grounded in men's violent control of women in ancient Near Eastern societies (1995: 318).

But, while patriarchy is clearly a common theme in Sanderson, Magdalene, and Thistlethwaite, Gordon and Washington explore in greater depth how the rhetoric of Nahum 3 relies upon a particular construction of male sexual desire.

Drawing on A. Richlin's 'Reading Ovid's Rapes', which demonstrates the poet's eroticization of military language, Gordon and Washington highlight how Nahum, too, fits the definition of 'pornographic'. Erotic pleasure and sexual violence are linked most clearly in 3.4-7, where Woman Nineveh who is raped before the gaze of onlookers is described as desirable, 'full of grace' (3.4):

> By implying that only the beautiful are raped, these texts treat rape as though it were the 'natural' result of male desire. This serves to disguise aggression as an act of 'love' and begins the process of placing the blame on the woman (1995: 319-20)

To Gordon and Washington's questions 'Why is there a woman in this picture? Why is she beautiful? And why is she guilty?' (p. 316), '[male] pornographic fantasy' is the logical answer.

Like the other commentators, Gordon and Washington advocate resistance to the language of Nahum 3. Their strategy, like that of Exum discussed above, is to refuse to identify with the male protagonist of the piece:

> Like Fetterley, we refuse to take that point of view...we accept neither the devastated woman as the appropriate representation of punishment, nor the conquered city as the licit object of military conquest. We reject the equation of bad women and bad cities, and we reject the idea that male violence (sexual and military) delivers just punishment (1995: 324).

To a patriarchal and pornographic Nahum, Gordon and Washington say 'No'.

5. *Evaluation of previous feminist treatments of Nahum*. These treatments are powerful in naming the violence of the text and in drawing the important connection between biblical metaphor and real-life violence against women. They recognize the need to resist abusive metaphors and the mentalities that undergird them, rather than attempting to deem the texts as 'only' metaphor.

Gordon and Washington are particularly helpful in focusing on patriarchy as a system. In so doing, they attempt to address a quandary that I raised in the commentary to Nahum 3: if Nahum is not using the marriage metaphor, then why is Yahweh concerned with Nineveh's promiscuity? Why is Yahweh punishing Nineveh? Gordon and Washington (and Bird to some degree) underscore that prostitution is a threat to patriarchy and that punishment of it is a system of male control.

Two significant gaps nonetheless remain in all of these treatments of gender in Nahum. First, all consider the violation of Woman Nineveh in Nahum 3 in isolation from the rest of the book. They do not account for the depiction of Judah or Thebes (other feminine characters)—or the construction of masculinity which is its logically—necessary pair. Second, none acknowledges the limitation of the 'Just say No' approach to Nineveh's rape, but they operate as if one could simply bracket out a sexist image from an otherwise acceptable book and Bible. None of these commentators (not even Gordon and Washington) deal in depth with the pervasiveness of patriarchy in the ancient texts and in the modern world—how as a system patriarchy informs the entire book and (as I will explore below) how such an essentialist understanding of women (and of men) itself inscribes the very patriarchy they claim to resist. Their single-minded effort to underscore the horror of the rape of Everywoman Nineveh in ch. 3 underestimates how pervasive patriarchal assumptions are in the book as a whole and, ironically, ignores the fact that the book offers the tools for its own deconstruction.

II. Nahum's Gender Project

Nahum 3 is not the only part of the book to employ gender, and Nineveh is not the only woman in Nahum. Rather, the book posits four primary characters, whose gender is important to their role: (1) Yahweh/ Nahum (masculine) who speaks *against* (2) Nineveh (feminine) and (3) the king of Assyria (masculine) and, once, *to* (4) Judah (feminine). A secondary character, Thebes (feminine), is mentioned in the course of a threat against Nineveh.

A. Woman

Through its characterization, Nahum defines the feminine in a particular way, and that definition is given shape by the delineation of both its type and its anti-type. Nineveh, who has received most attention from feminist commentators, constitutes in Nahum the anti-type of the female. Nineveh is a whore, promiscuous, a woman who is no one's property and whose sexuality is not an instrument in the service of patriarchy.

Contrapuntal to the anti-type Nineveh, Judah is the ideal feminine. Her safety is not guaranteed but clearly controlled by the will of her governing male: 'I have afflicted you; I will afflict you no more' (1.12). Neither her crimes nor her characteristics are named. Indeed, her vindication restores honor not to herself but to the male—'because Yahweh has returned the pride of Jacob' (2.3).

On the one hand, these distinctions pit women against one another. Judah is not only contrasted with but threatened by the example of Nineveh: see what happens when one does not take refuge in Yahweh? The example of Thebes, the woman already ravished (3.8), threatens not only Nineveh but Judah as well: no physical surroundings were strong enough to protect *her* from devastation. Unlike the promiscuous woman (Nineveh) and the woman who trusted her home for protection (Thebes), the good woman (Judah) with her male protector is safe.

On the other hand, both the type and the anti-type construct a single definition of the female. Women find their only protection in a male in whom they find refuge. To be beautiful and promiscuous or to trust in one's own security is to invite shame and invasive violence.

B. Man

In the gender construction of the female, the male is also defined. If femaleness means vulnerability and the need to rely on the protection of the male, then maleness is known as strength, power, and the ability to protect one's women. As in the case of femininity, this construction of masculinity is shaped in Nahum by the depiction of type and anti-type.

The king of Assyria stands as the masculine anti-type. As we saw in the commentary, the closing verses of Nahum link the previously unidentified male pronouns with the king: he is not only the enemy of Yahweh (1.2) but also the recipient of the threats and taunts that end each chapter. At the close of Nahum 1, his is the rod that will be broken (1.13); he is the one who will lose procreative power (1.14); and his is the grave that will be set (1.14). At the close of Nahum 2, he is the one represented by the lion in the short allegory: in a strikingly domestic understanding of the lion's den, he is the male once able to protect and provide for his women and his children (2.13) but now stripped of those abilities by Yahweh. At the close of Nahum 3, he is the one who is taunted, and his is the wound that is incurable (3.19). Throughout, the male king is threatened with and taunted for failing in his primary role: that of protecting his woman.

In the course of depicting the king of Assyria as the male anti-type, Nahum constructs the ideal masculinity of Yahweh. Yahweh, the Divine Warrior, is ultimate in power and strength: he protects those who take refuge in him (1.7); he retains the right both to afflict and to protect Judah (1.12); he cuts off another's procreative ability (1.14); he overpowers armies. Centrally, it is also Yahweh who rapes Nineveh.

Though Gordon and Washington posit that Yahweh acts to control the unattached woman who threatens patriarchy, a holistic look at the book's construction of gender suggests that God rapes Nineveh not because of her crimes but as a means of humiliating the male who was supposed to protect her. The Lion-King who once provided a safe den, with no one to frighten (2.12), now must watch along with others (3.5) as Woman Nineveh is ravaged. Perhaps the rape of Nineveh in 3.4-7 is the king's 'wound', his 'incurable breach' (3.19). Or perhaps it is hers.

C. The Patriarchal Shape-box

As with a child's shape-sorting box, the contours into which Nahum has molded masculinity and femininity slide effortlessly into the box called 'patriarchy'—they are blocks made for and by an ideology of male control and protectionism. Nahum reflects and constructs a world in which women's sexuality is controlled by men and in which men are valued for their ability to maintain that control.

As previous feminist commentators aptly have discerned, this patriarchal ideology provides the necessary backdrop for the rape of Nineveh in Nahum 3. Brownmiller's classic study of the patriarchal ideology of rape insists that, especially in war, rape of women is the ultimate means by which to humiliate the men who perceive themselves as protectors:

> Defense of women has long been a hallmark of masculine pride, as possession of women has been a hallmark of masculine success... The body of a raped woman becomes a ceremonial battlefield, a parade ground for the victor's trooping of the colors. The act that is played out upon her is a message passed between men—vivid proof of victory for one and loss and defeat for the others (Brownmiller 1975: 31).

Rape of women is as much about men as it is about women themselves.

But the feminist commentators I have surveyed fail to take this general insight further to see that in Nahum the males engaged in a battle of honor are named. Yahweh sexually humiliates Nineveh not out of a concern for Woman Nineveh nor out of a general commitment to patriarchy.

Rather, rape of Nineveh is the ultimate disgrace of Assyria's king, the lion who could not protect his den. The battle is one for honor between males, transacted on the bodies of their women. Assyria had humiliated Judah (feminine), so Yahweh now humiliates Nineveh (feminine).

These commentators also have failed to see how all the characters of the book are constructed according to the template of the same patriarchal shape-box. Nineveh is not the only character gendered in Nahum: so, too, are Judah, Thebes, the king of Assyria, and Yahweh. Each has a shaped hole into which it is designed to fall.

III. Deconstructive Possibilities

Gender construction is clearly one of Nahum's primary rhetorical strategies. Cast as females, Judah, Nineveh, and Thebes become vulnerable, in need of protection; unless Judah takes refuge in and remains faithful to Yahweh the Warrior, she will suffer Nineveh's (and Thebes') fate—rape. But Nahum's rhetoric of rape often falters in its consistency. Like patriarchy itself, its very attempt at total domination cannot bear the strain.

A. Unite and Conquer

I have argued that the social control of patriarchy pits women against each other. In order to avoid both stigma and personal harm, a woman must distance herself from women who eschew male control. The brutal treatment afforded the promiscuous Nineveh and the futility of Thebes's self-defense communicate a clear, consistent point to Judah: to be safe requires male protection/control. In introducing the case of Thebes, however, Nahum invites identification among women.

The logic of Nah. 3.8-11 depends on Nineveh imagining herself like Thebes: 'Are you better than Thebes…? Even she [went] into exile… Also you will become drunk…' Nahum invites Nineveh (and Judah) to experience Thebes's pain, to care about her exile.

In the service of Nahum's rhetoric, the mutual identification of the females helps reinforce their dependence (all women need male protection) and it also feeds female fear. Just as Nineveh is reminded that what happened to Thebes can happen to her, so, too, as Brownmiller describes, stories of the rape of others lead real-life women to control themselves and to reign in their own independence. And yet, in challenge to Nahum's rhetoric, the identification among women also challenges the good woman–bad woman dichotomy on which patriarchy depends. Any sympathy or empathy that the 'good woman' feels for the 'bad woman' erodes the distinction between them. Once Nineveh can empathize with Thebes, there is nothing to keep Judah from empathizing with Nineveh.

Hence, in one way, the contemporary feminist choice to read with Nineveh, to refuse to demonize her or to exult over her rape, is a theoretical move suggested by the complications of the text's own rhetoric. And yet ironically the feminist strategy of reading with Nineveh runs the risk of simply reversing the good woman–bad woman dichotomy in Nahum. When Nineveh becomes the sole focus of discussion, when only her status is redefined, Judah's own identity is challenged. In a world without whores, what defines a good woman? And when self-determination becomes the mark of the heroine, does Judah become the bad woman?

A deconstructive reading of Nahum, then, goes further than a simple 'Identify-with-Nineveh' approach and recognizes that the call for Nineveh and Judah to identify with Thebes undercuts distinctions between women that are based on whether or not they have a male protector. Indeed, solidarity among women in Nahum comes from their recognition that all women—the good as well as the bad—have been or are waiting to be hurt by patriarchy. Things change when 'Who will grieve Nineveh?' (3.7) is no longer a rhetorical question but one with an answer: Judah.

B. The Lingering Male

Several clues in the book of Nahum have suggested that feminine imagery in Nahum is instrumental rather than fundamental; the construction of the feminine serves to communicate to males. The book's male focus is made clear throughout the book's structure: each chapter ends with a threat and/or taunt of a male; the enigmatic but persistent male pronouns keep the male in the reader's mind; and the book ends not with the rape of Nineveh but with the taunt of the male, now identified as the king of Assyria. Ideologically, Nahum 3 describes rape in classical patriarchal terms: Yahweh's rape of Nineveh is not punishment for her unfaithfulness to him (as in the prophetic marriage metaphor) but a means by which the Assyrian king is shamed in front of others.

Judith Butler's *Bodies that Matter: On the Discursive Limits of 'Sex'* (1993) argues that underlying the ideology of male protectionism is anxiety over male lack. If by definition masculinity means power and femininity means vulnerability, then linguistically and ideologically no space remains for the frightful possibility that men can suffer trauma or loss. No men have the phallus (Lacan's term for absolute power), but without it men lose their identity as males; they are not real men but women, 'girlie boys'. According to Butler (1993: 205), the vulnerable female becomes the image not only of what men fear becoming but also of what they know themselves already to be:

> The masculine anxiety over loss denotes an impossibility of having, an always already having lost the phallus which makes the 'having' into an impossible ideal, and approximates the phallus as the deferral of that having, a having to have that is never had. The having of the phallus as the site of anxiety is already the loss that it fears, and it is this recognition of the masculine implication in abjection that the feminine serves to defer.

As Burlein notes, popular culture attempts to manage this masculine 'crisis' in action-adventure films and men's pulp fiction. By projecting male lack onto women, these fantasies teach that men do not fall short; it is women who lack strength and need protection.

Nahum *consciously* utilizes these dynamics in its taunt of the king of Assyria. His masculinity is challenged directly (he cannot fulfill the role of the male lion to protect his den) and indirectly (where is he while Nineveh is raped?). His warriors are feminized: they are 'women in your midst' (3.13), their 'gates' opened wide (see the commentary on Nah. 3 for the sexual connotations). By the end of the book, the king is rhetorically feminized as well: he receives the same taunts and rhetorical questions in 3.19 as were addressed to Nineveh in 3.7.

At the same time, such rhetoric also affects the characterization of Yahweh. If Nineveh serves in Nahum as the site of (Assyrian) male anxiety, what about the other male and female pair—Judah and her God? When read through Butler's analysis, Nah. 1.12 takes on enormous weight: 'I have afflicted you, I will afflict you no more.' In a book where the definition of maleness is the protection of the female, Yahweh admits he has not taken care of Judah. How, then, is he different from the king of Assyria who has not protected his female?

Many commentators attempt to erase this apparent problem by suggesting that Nahum follows the book of Isaiah in discerning divine control in both Assyria's defeat of Israel/Judah *and* in Assyria's own demise. *After* God uses Assyria as the 'rod of my anger' (Isa. 10.5) then the rod, too, will be punished. 'When Yahweh has finished all his work on Mount Zion and on Jerusalem, he will punish the arrogant boasting of the king of Assyria and his haughty pride' (Isa. 10.12). If Nahum were following the same logic of Isaiah, Yahweh's admission that he had afflicted Judah would not challenge his masculine abilities to protect but rather would underscore his power to determine Judah's fate.

Nahum's attribution of Assyrian oppression of Judah to God's doing, however, is more subtle. Importantly, Nahum never makes the connection explicit. As my discussion on Nah. 1.1 explored, Nahum does not share Isaiah's concern to outline Judah's sins that led to her initial punishment or the change in circumstance that now calls for a different divine response. Nonetheless, literary clues in 1.11-14 *do* link Yahweh's affliction of Judah with Assyrian oppression. Immediately after Yahweh's announcement that 'I will afflict you no more', he proclaims, 'I will break his rod from upon you' (1.13). This masculine singular pronoun, as I argued, is linked with the masculine figure in 1.14, which in turn is identified as the king of Assyria in the final verses of the book. That is, 'I will afflict you no more', in the combined rhetoric of the book, is synonymous with 'I will break his rod from upon you'. Nahum intimates what Isaiah makes explicit: Yahweh's hand guided Judah's subjugation to the Assyrians.

The ideology of male protectionism that pervades the book of Nahum also draws attention to the laconic nature of 1.12. Its attempt at a quick answer highlights a question that has gone unraised in the book: if maleness is defined as the ability to protect the female and if the subjugation of the enemy's female is the means of asserting power, then does not Judah's own subjugation by the Assyrians challenge Yahweh's masculinity? The implicit problem that drives the book (the affliction of Judah at the hands of Yahweh's enemy) itself raises male anxiety. Can Yahweh really be a man if Judah is humiliated, especially when Nineveh's rape de-masculinizes the king of Assyria? Rather than answering the problem, 1.12 calls attention to its own deceptive simplicity: in its efforts at a quick fix, it reminds the reader of a problem that Nahum has not addressed. What kind of man is Yahweh to let Judah be humiliated in the first place?

In turn, Nahum's attempt to hypermasculinize Yahweh becomes suspect as well. The book's opening, with its over-the-top, earth-shattering vision of the Divine Warrior against whom no one can stand and its repeated threats against the king of Assyria, mask male anxiety. They attempt to shield Yahweh from the threat to his honor and might that the Assyrian defeat of Judah has posed.

Tellingly, most commentators on Nahum define the goal of the book as defending God's power and might. So, Christensen (1988: 736-38): 'Nahum is primarily a book about God's justice, not about human vengeance, hatred, and military conquest.' And Peels (1995: 201, 278; my italics):

> With the mention of the patience of God in vs. 3a, along with the words 'great in power', it is not the paradox of salvation/destruction that is introduced, but rather the troubling question is raised why God, who is the Avenger, has to this point left the injustice uncorrected. God's long-suffering relates to his patience, not powerlessness: He has postponed the judgment, but not neglected it... If it is said of this God, who is King, that He

98 Nahum and (Wo)men

> avenges himself, this can no longer be considered to be indicative of an evil humour, a tyrannical capriciousness, or an eruption of rancour. God's vengeance is kingly vengeance. If He takes vengeance, He does so as the highest authority exercising punishing justice. The vengeance of God is the action of God-as-King in the realization of his sovereign rule. This action is directed against those who offend God's majesty *through transgression against his honour, his justice* or his people.

And Robinson (1952: 114): 'It is not Israel's pride that is at stake but God's honor; and it is not even the redemption of the people that is primary, but the vindication of their God.'

These three commentators recognize that Nahum attempts to defend Yahweh's (masculine) power against all challenges, though they fail to take into account how those challenges are raised by the rhetoric of the book of Nahum itself.

C. De-essentializing Gender

1. *The trouble with gender.* Thus far I have mapped the contours of Nahum's gender scripts. What links Nineveh, Judah, and Thebes together is their inability to protect themselves, their dependence on another to defend them. Yahweh's rape of Nineveh is not the punishment of an unfaithful wife but the humiliation of the king of Assyria, the lion who is unable to protect his den. Maleness is conterminous with the ability to protect; femaleness, with vulnerability.

Recognizing this aspect of Nahum's use of gender is important not only for understanding the book's rhetoric, but also for the cause of feminist agency. As I have maintained, feminists who focus only on the rape of Nineveh in Nahum 3 underestimate the power of gender to shape the entire book. The gender ideology of Nahum—and its feminist interpreters—runs deeper still.

In *Bodies that Matter* and in *Gender Trouble: Feminism and the Subversion of Identity* (1990), Butler argues that the binary distinction between male and female itself serves the ideological purposes of heterosexual hegemony (and, thus, by extension patriarchy). Disputing classic feminists who contrast 'gender' (defined as societal expectations) and 'sex' (defined as biological given), Butler argues that 'sex' itself is a discursively constructed category. Language regulates and regularizes bodies; the differences and 'insignificant' parts of bodies are marginalized to force humans to fit a male or female template. Butler argues that bodies are not simply born as male or female; rather, the societal gaze sculpts them into conformity: ' "becoming" a gender is a laborious process of becoming *naturalized*, which requires a differentiation of bodily pleasures and parts on the basis of gendered meanings' (1993: 70). The

conformity of bodies to a singular 'sex' is fundamental for the function-
ing of patriarchy. Only if a society agrees what constitutes a female (or a
male) can it perpetually reinscribe gender expectations.

Butler (1993: 147) maintains that challenging heterosexual hierarchy
(which I am equating with patriarchy) requires the challenging of foundationalist notions of male and female.

> The identity categories often presumed to be foundational to feminist poli-
> tics, that is deemed necessary in order to mobilize feminism as an identity
> politics, simultaneously work to limit and constrain in advance the very
> cultural possibilities that feminism is supposed to open up.

When women accept a unified definition of woman, they corroborate
with the patriarchal ideology that defines women's and men's roles.

2. *Essentialized gender in Nahum*. The book of Nahum not only relies
upon foundationalist notions of sex, the presumption that 'male' and
'female' are stable, immutable categories, but it also represents the
female body accordingly. Nahum 3, for example, identifies Nineveh as
woman according to her genitals. She is first called a whore, a term
which not only reinforces patriarchy via its injunction that women's
sexuality be exclusive and controlled by males, but which also defines
Nineveh by her sexuality. In turn, when Nineveh is humiliated, what is
seen is not her face (covered by her skirts) but her nakedness (paralleled
with 'shame'). Her vulnerability is sexual vulnerability, the reality that
her body can be displayed to others, ravaged, against her will. Nahum
3.13 makes the same point: when soldiers become 'women in your
midst', their 'gates' are opened wide. With femaleness thus described,
the invisible bodies of Judah and Thebes become sexed as well, and the
nature of their vulnerability also becomes genital.

That this sexing of the female body is rhetorically significant and not
just a 'natural' by-product of language is underscored by the instances in
which bodies are *not* sexed in Nahum. In Nah. 3.3, for example, the
bodies of the slain are anonymous, generic. Although grammatically the
Hebrew word for 'corpse' is feminine, Nahum does not dissect the
bodies that are tossed around, literally and literarily, in 3.3. Only the
female body is marked as sexed.

Male bodies receive little attention in Nahum. In the Divine Warrior
hymn in Nahum 1, we hear of Yahweh's feet (his power to crush) and of
the length of his nose (his slowness to anger), though we never are
offered an image that would correspond to the look at Nineveh's genitals. Nonetheless, the phallus is not absent from Nahum. If a woman is
defined as the one who can be genitally penetrated, and if only two

options for sex are allowed, then the male becomes by definition the who can enter her—the one with the invasive penis.

As Butler (1993: 45) traces in psychological terms, the absence of the phallus in women is necessary for the definition of what it means to be male:

> That process of meaning-constitution requires that women reflect that masculine power and everywhere reassure that power of the reality of its illusory autonomy. This task is confounded, to say the least, when the demands that women reflect the autonomous power of masculine subject/signifier becomes essential to the construction of that autonomy and, thus, becomes the basis of a radical dependency that effectively undercuts the function it serves. But further, this dependency, though denied, is also *pursued* by the masculine subject…[in order to be] the reflector and guarantor of an apparent masculine subject position, women must become, must 'be' (in the sense of 'posture as if they were') precisely what men are not and, in their very lack, establish the essential function of men.

In Nahum, men need women in order to be men. Yahweh and the king of Assyria depend upon Nineveh, Judah, and Thebes for their identity. Without her vulnerability, why would Judah need Yahweh? Without Nineveh's openness to invasion, how would Yahweh re-establish that he can protect Judah and thus fulfill his role as a real man?

3. *Essentialized gender in feminist commentaries on Nahum.* Perhaps even more strikingly than does the book itself, feminist commentators also have relied upon an essentialist understanding of sex. Despite their admirable intention of challenging the gender ideologies of biblical depictions of violence against women, through their choice to side hermeneutically with the woman in the text feminist interpreters accept the immutable category of 'woman' and also implicitly the identity that patriarchy crafts for her.

For example, Exum's (1995: 265) powerful critique of the gender ideology of the prophetic books begins with the basic premise (summarized at the beginning of this chapter) that women readers automatically read the texts in particular ways:

> Our 'natural' identification lies with the sinful, humiliated woman. This situation, as I said at the beginning of this essay, forces women readers to read against our own interests and to accept the indictment of our sex encoded in these texts. Male readers, in contrast, are not reading against their interests when they adopt God's point of view toward the sinful woman. On the contrary, it is against their interests to stay in the humiliating female subject position.

In what Exum deems 'natural', Butler discerns the success of patriarchal hegemony: the ideology of patriarchy trains certain humans to identify themselves as women and hence to identify with the experience of and threat against all humans labeled women. In an ironic and dangerous way, Exum's acceptance of this identity accepts patriarchy's insistence that all women are the same—and, more to the point, concurs that what makes women women is their ability to be raped. A simple reversal of the values of the text, to grant value to women's sexual autonomy against Nahum's punishment of it, clearly goes only so far in critiquing the patriarchal assumptions of the book. Nineveh is only treated like a sister because she, like us, can be raped.

An easy identification with any of the figures in the book of Nahum—Nineveh or Judah, the king of Assyria or Yahweh—accepts the gender scripts that define them. To choose to stand with the female characters of Nahum offers no real liberation: to identify with Nineveh is to define oneself as a victim, or someone who is afraid of being a victim; to identify with Judah is to define oneself as someone grateful to be rescued by a strong, comforting arm. A choice to read with the male is no less comforting; to identify with the king of Assyria is to identify with one whose masculinity is defined by his power and to identify with Yahweh is to identify with one whose very identity depends on the just workings of the world. No politics of identification can challenge the patriarchal system on which Nahum's definitions of sex and gender depend.

Sanderson, too, offers a necessary and valuable appraisal of the patriarchal logic of Nahum, but, like Exum, essentializes 'woman'. She takes for granted that modern readers will read according to their gender, that the gender of the characters in Nahum corresponds in a self-evident way to the gender of modern persons:

> What would it mean to worship a God who is portrayed as raping women when angry?… To involve God in an image of sexual violence is, in a profound way, somehow to justify it and thereby to sanction it for human males who are for any reason angry with a woman… It is dangerous enough that God is depicted as male while human beings are female. The danger is greatly compounded when God is depicted as a male who proves his manhood and superiority through violent and sexual retaliation against women (1992: 221).

Sanderson is right in seeing that Nahum's essentialist understanding of gender converges with current essentialist understandings of gender to create a dangerous matrix: Nahum's gender ideology seems so dangerous because it is so familiar. What Sanderson does not acknowledge, however, is that to continue to position women as the opposite of men is to perpetuate patriarchy's insistence on a heterosexual norm.

4. *Alternatives to gender*. Butler's 'answer' to the patriarchal inscription of gender and the sex on which it depends does not deny the category of gender altogether; she acknowledges that, discursively and politically, one cannot talk as if gender does not exist. She argues instead (1993: 19, 145) that gender systems offer the means of their own demise; like language in general, gender systems cannot control the multiplicity of their meanings, and ultimately they deconstruct themselves:

> Because texts do not reflect the entirety of their authors or their worlds, they enter a field of reading as partial provocations, not only requiring a set of prior texts in order to gain legibility, but–at best–initiating a set of appropriations and criticisms that call into question their fundamental premises... The coexistence or convergence of such discursive injunctions produces the possibility of a complex reconfiguration and redeployment... There is only a taking of the tools where they lie, where the very 'taking up' is enabled by the tool lying there.

That is, gender identity comes with a such a laundry list of requirements that the requirements themselves become not only contradictory but also amenable to reassembly into new configurations. The tools at hand can be used in new ways.

Nahum clearly identifies femaleness with sexual vulnerability; to be a woman is to be one whose site of 'shame' (3.5) can be displayed and penetrated against her will. The only mitigation for such vulnerability is the protection of a male. And yet, Nahum also recognizes other features of womanhood. In Nah. 3.4, a woman can be a harlot, one who not only escapes male control but does so at the desire of men; her refusal to be owned by a single man, despite its challenge to patriarchal hegemony, pleases many males. Nahum 3.4 also recognizes the power of the harlot. Appealing to men, she controls them. Rather than the object who is bought and sold, she is the agent who 'sells nations by her harlotries'. She controls men so completely that it can only be due to sorcery.

Clearly, it is the harlot's control over men that Yahweh seeks to punish, and yet in acknowledging Nineveh's power, the very definition of woman as vulnerable is challenged. If in 3.4 Nineveh has the phallus, the means of control, then the definition of male as protector is challenged. While the manhood of the king of Assyria is challenged explicitly by the book, the very definition of manhood is challenged implicitly by the power Nineveh exerts in 3.4.

Such an argument that gender as a category is deconstructable in the book of Nahum, suggestive rather than exhaustive, is not intended to denigrate previous feminist critique of the book nor to dismantle a platform from which to exercise feminist agency. Rather, exposing the discursive structures that circumscribe female and male identities and lives offers an alternative, and more subversive, means by which to resist the oppression of women.

IV. Conclusion: The Patriarchal Fishbowl

In her discussion of the cultural underpinnings that mainstream culture shares with the racist right, Ann Burlein (2002: 196) evokes Toni Morrison's image of the fishbowl. Describing her sudden realization of the pervasiveness of racism, Morrison (1992: 46) recounts:

> It is as if I had been looking at the fishbowl—the glide and flick of the golden scales, the green tip, the bolt of white careening back from the gills; the castles at the bottom, surrounded by pebbles and tiny, intricate fronds of green; the barely disturbed water, the flecks of waste and food, the tranquil bubbles traveling to the surface—and suddenly I saw the bowl, the structure that transparently (and invisibly) permits the life it contains to exist in the larger world.

In a similar way, an exploration of 'gender trouble' raised by Judith Butler's analysis suggests that the standard feminist calls to 'Just say No' to the violence against women in Nahum 3 do not go far enough in naming the structure that holds it, invisibly, in place. In Nahum patriarchy is not only operative in the portrait of Nineveh's rape in ch. 3; it permeates every pore of the book—the treatment of the king of Assyria, and, perhaps even more importantly, the description of Yahweh the Protector and Defender of Judah. Ironically, feminist advocacy against the rape of and violence against women in Nahum has inadequately recognized how the entire book—and, indeed, how the entire culture of its interpreters—all swim within the confines of the patriarchal fishbowl.

The book of Nahum is permeated with patriarchy, but so is the culture in which I write and work and, perhaps more importantly, the self-image and values that I have internalized, the very things that often feel most 'normal' and 'natural'. Patriarchy is too big for anyone to 'Just say No'. But a reading along the lines of Butler suggests that even—and perhaps especially—in the most thoroughgoing patriarchy, new permutations, new ways of being and living are possible.

Nahum and Atrocity

> Perhaps we cannot prevent this world from being a world in which
> children are tortured. But we can reduce the number of tortured children
> (Camus 1961: 73; quoted in Ellis 1997: 190).

I. Introduction

In the previous chapter I argued that patriarchal ideology in the book of
Nahum cannot be contained by a simple feminist 'No': it is the invisible
fishbowl that provides the book with its shape. Resistence to the gender
messages of Nahum is possible, however, when readers recognize their
ability to 'pick up the tools where they lie' and use them in new ways;
the internal inconsistences within the list of requirements for 'true'
woman and 'true' man offer the invitation to reassemble its items in
alternative, subversive ways.

Similarly, in this chapter I shall suggest the inadequacy of both a
simple 'No' and an easy 'Yes' to the violence of the book of Nahum. The
violence of Nahum, like the patriarchy with which it is interwoven, runs
throughout the rhetorical logic of the book and throughout the culture
of the commentators who attempt to distance themselves from it. I shall
also explore the complex interplay between book's violent manifest
content and its artistic literary style, suggesting that the book's art both
undergirds and undercuts its rage.

II. The Problem of Nahum

As I have traced in the previous chapters, feminist interpreters have seen
the treatment of Woman Nineveh in ch. 3 as the hallmark of Nahum's
violence. A woman figure is called a whore, her genitals exposed and her
body mistreated, while others are goaded to watch and taunt. This
'pornoprophetic' image which intertwines violence and sex epitomizes,
for feminists, the horror of the book.

In the history of the book's interpretation, though, discussions of the
book's violence rarely have mentioned the rape of Nineveh, highlighting
the striking difference that gender and gender awareness make in reading. In 1947, for example, the 'moral offense' of Nahum 3 to which Raymond Calkins devotes several pages is not its violence against women
but rather its frankness of language. Expressing a sentiment that will be
echoed below, he explains (p. 82): 'We are justly reminded that there

exists a well-marked difference between Oriental and Western habits of thought and language with respect to matters of sex.' Similarly, C. von Orelli (1893: 233) finds nothing wrong with the punishment of Nineveh in Nah. 3.5; it is the 'insulting treatment such as an unchaste woman merits'. In fact, I have found no discussion of the book prior to 1950 that singles out Nineveh's rape as an example of the book's violence.

Rather, most commentators have lambasted Nahum for its fascination with war and the glee with which it calls for revenge. Graphic depictions of the siege of Nineveh in 2.4-11; 3.1-3; and 3.12-15 describe war in its bloody detail.

> Plunder silver, plunder gold! But there is no end to the measurement! Abundance of every precious vessel! Emptiness and void and waste! And heart melts and knees totter and anguish in all loins! (Nah. 2.11)

> Horse lifting up and blade of sword and spear flashing and a multitude slain and abundance of corpse and no end to the corpse, and they stumble over their bodies (Nah. 3.3).

War is not just narrated, but narrated gleefully, tauntingly:

> You also will be drunken, you will go into hiding; you will seek a refuge from the enemy. All your fortresses are like fig trees with first-ripe figs—if shaken they fall into the mouth of the eater. Look at your troops. They are women in your midst. The gates of your land are wide open to your foes; fire has devoured the bars of your gates. Draw water for the siege, strengthen your forts; trample the clay, tread the mortar, take hold of the brick mold! There the fire will devour you, the sword will cut you off. It will devour you like the locust (Nah. 3.11-15).

Throughout, Nahum resolutely refuses any empathy or care for those about to be destroyed:

> Nineveh is devastated; who will bemoan her? Where shall I seek comforters for you? (Nah. 3.7)

> There is no assuaging your hurt, your wound is mortal. All who hear the news about you clap their hands over you (Nah. 3.19).

Nahum does not merely describe war and its toil; it revels in imagining the panic and death of the Assyrian foe.

III. Responses to Nahum's Violence

What does a reader *make of*—and what does a reader *do with*—a book single-mindedly devoted to calling for and rejoicing in the violent death of the enemy? This section will explore how various commentators have responded to Nahum's violence and will offer some analysis of their efforts.

A. Response 1: No

1. *Nahum the nationalistic poet.* For many nineteenth- and twentieth-century readers, the violence of Nahum decisively demonstrated that it is a morally inferior book, one that civilized persons should eschew. Such a response was especially common among Christian commentators prior to 1950, who saw Nahum's nationalism and desire for vengeance as the very antithesis to the loving, forgiving spirit of a universal Christianity.

While this response to Nahum was widespread, I focus on four representative samples:

James Cleland (1956: 957):

> His [Nahum's] God is a throwback to the Yahweh of battles of the early days of the kingdom. He is a militant nationalist as he infers that Judah is not as other nations, especially Assyria...[but] Nahum may be redeemed. Nahum need not be the norm; Jesus may be. The remedy for Nahum is a simple and drastic one. It is no more or less than a change of heart, a fundamental conversion in terms of Jesus's view of God and man.

J.M.P. Smith (1911):

> To a Semitic people, tenacious of revenge, the downfall of an ancient tyrant would be an occasion for joyous celebration long after release from the tyranny had been realised (p. 277).

> Nahum was an enthusiastic, optimistic patriot...[his work] exhibits a degree of animosity for which the great ethical prophets furnish no parallel. The pent-up feelings of generations of suffering patriots here burst forth into flame. The whole prophecy is a paean of triumph over a prostrate foe and breathes out the pursuit of exultant revenge... In Nahum, a representative of the old, narrow and shallow prophetism finds its place in the Canon of Scripture. The possibility that new occasions might teach new duties, that the advancing civilisation with its more complex life might render the old usages and laws inadequate, and that Yahweh might care more for full justice and overflowing mercy than for the blood of bulls and goats had not been realised by them... Patriotism and religion combined in requiring the belief that Yahweh was able and willing to deliver his people out of every danger... The overthrow of Nineveh not only brought to Nahum and those of like mind satisfaction of the natural, human desire for vengeance, but it also enabled them to justify the ways of God to men (pp. 280-82).

G.A. Smith (1903: 91-92):

> For he [Nahum] represents no single movement of his fickle people's progress, but the passion of the whole epoch then drawing to a close... Such is the sheer religion of the Proem to the Book of Nahum—thoroughly Oriental in its sense of God's method and resources of destruction; very Jewish, and very natural to that age of Jewish history, in the bursting of its

long pent hopes of revenge. We of the West might express these hopes
differently. We should not attribute so much personal passion to the
Avenger. With our keener sense of law, we should emphasise the slowness
of the process.

Raymond Calkins (1947: 84):

> We who have been trained in the Christian idea of God, and in Jesus'
> teaching that love must extend even to our enemies, must remember that
> [when we read Nahum] we are still in the Old Testament. The moral
> education of God's people was not complete. For the Hebrews, it was as
> natural to hate one's enemies as to love one's friends.

Although Calkins does find something redeemable in Nahum, namely
the idea of righteous anger, he shares with the commentators spot-
lighted here the notion that the call for the downfall of the enemy is a
Hebrew and not a Christian value.

For these and other authors of the early twentieth century, the nar-
rowness of Nahum becomes especially evident when contrasted to the
witness of other prophetic books. Not only is Nahum the antithesis of
the book of Jonah, which parodies the parochialism and jingoism of the
people and offers Nineveh (successfully, at that) the opportunity to
repent, but also it contravenes the nature of 'ethical prophets' who focus
on the sins of their own people:

> The contrast between the message of Nahum and that of Jeremiah, his con-
> temporary, is striking. To the prophet of larger vision and deeper insight,
> the event which filled Nahum's entire range of vision was of relatively
> slight importance… Instead of grieving over the sin of Judah… Nahum was
> apparently content to lead her in a jubilant celebration of the approaching
> death of Assyria. Jeremiah was too overwhelmed by sorrow and alarm for
> his own people to obtain any solace from the misfortune of another, which
> could bring no relief to the desperate situation of Judah (J.M.P. Smith
> 1911: 281).

In these commentaries Nahum's most grievous sin is the failure to call
Judah accountable for its own sin—in turning the word of God against
the nations while remaining silent about those of his own people,
Nahum fails to adopt the normative role of the prophet:

> Zephaniah had also doomed the Assyrian capital, yet he was much more
> concerned with Israel's unworthiness of the opportunity presented to
> them… For this Nahum had no thought. His heart, for all its bigness, holds
> room only for the bitter memories, the baffled hopes, the unappeased
> hatreds of a hundred years (G.A. Smith 1903: 90)

> [Nahum] exhibits a degree of animosity for which the great ethical prophets
> furnish no parallel (J.M.P. Smith 1911: 280).

'Ethical' prophets, it seems, only announce the death of their own people.

Even as late as 1993, Brian Peckham (p. 406) would complain:

> There is no mention at all of Judah's or Jerusalem's guilt [in Nahum], of the things that its kings, princes, prophets, or people did wrong. The book of Nahum came after the Deuteronomistic History, knew its historical and theological theories, and obviously did not agree with them at all or pay them any mind.

Although these commentators find Nahum morally offensive, they are unable to deny the book's poetic art. 'While Nahum is a worse prophet than Zephaniah, with less conscience and less insight, he is a greater poet' (G.A. Smith 1903: 91).

For these reasons, Mary Ellen Chase (1952: 179-81, quoted in Preminger and Greenstein 1986: 505-506) denied Nahum the label 'prophet' and deemed him instead a 'nationalistic poet':

> Place he surely deserves and the highest of recognition, but as a poet and not as a prophet... A complete and confirmed nationalist, he hated the 'bloody city' of Nineveh... It is a poem of bloodshed and horror, of vengeance and destruction, with little to relieve its savagery and violence; but it must be admired for the sheer power and force of its expression and for its awful, but brilliant imagery.

Nahum, according to these interpreters, is a violent, nationalistic book, one morally repugnant to modern persons. Its moral inferiority, however, does not mask its literary artistry. Nahum is a bad book written well.

2. Analysis
i. *Nationalism as an Oriental trait.* In their attempts to distance themselves from Nahum's violence, these commentators assume a particular type of Christian theology, one that posits Christianity as a universal religion, one predicated on forgiveness, not on revenge. They sharply contrast the theology of ancient Israel, which they see as nationalistic, exclusivist, and bound to the land, to that of Christianity, which they depict as engaging the heart and not national interests.

Such stereotypes of Judaism and Christianity both depend upon and fuel a supersessionist Christianity, one that ignores its own violence and concern for land while projecting them onto the Other and that also reads selectively the witness of the Hebrew Bible. (Though, to be fair, at least one Jewish commentator has made similar remarks. See Lipiński 1971: 795.) Jewish and Christian theologians of the twentieth century have drawn devastating connections between such views and the mentalities that enabled the Holocaust. Indeed, as we shall see below, Christian treatments of Nahum since the Holocaust have been more empathetic toward the book and insist that Nahum *must not* be contrasted negatively with the New Testament.

In the authors I have surveyed here, a supersessionist Christianity is interwoven with and indistinguishable from cultural imperialism. The quotation from G.A. Smith given above from *The Expositor's Bible* demonstrates clearly the dual 'othering' of the sentiments of Nahum; the call for the violent death of an oppressor is marked not only as 'Jewish' but also 'Oriental'.

In *Orientalism*, Edward Said gives a scathing critique of the ideological interests that created 'orientalism' as a field of study—the way in which colonial powers, especially from Napoleon onward, have shaped the lands they conquered into a stable, passive, mysterious Orient, the entity to stand as the 'great complementary opposite' (1979: 58) to their own 'advanced' societies:

> As a system of thought Orientalism approaches a heterogeneous, dynamic, and complex human reality from an uncritically essentialist standpoint; this suggests both an enduring Oriental reality and an opposing but not less enduring Western essence, which observes the Orient from afar and from, so to speak, above (Said 1979: 333).

The need to 'fix' the Orient, to ossify its traits and mentalities, is requisite for 'Western' identity and integrity. Orientalism, according to Said, is 'an accomplice to empire' (1979: 333).

Imperial interests are not far below the surface in the treatment of Nahum in *The Expositor's Bible*. Not only does Smith follow his denigration of nationalism as 'Oriental' with an extended excursus on the British empire but also he does so in a way that underscores just how 'Western' nationalism can be:

> The swift decay of these ancient empires [Assyria and Babylonia] from the climax of their commercial glory is often employed as a warning to ourselves. But the parallel...is very far from exact. If we can lay aside for the moment the greatest difference of all, in religion and morals, there remain others almost of cardinal importance. Assyria and Babylonia were not filled, like Great Britain, with reproductive races, able to colonise distant lands, and carry everywhere the spirit which had made them strong at home. Still more, they did not continue at home to be homogeneous... Their populations, especially in their capitals, were very largely alien and distraught, with nothing to hold them together save their commercial interest. They were bound to break up at the first disaster. It is true that we are not without some risks of their period. No patriot among us can observe without misgiving the large and growing proportion of foreigners in that department of our life from which the strength of our defence is largely drawn–

our merchant navy. But...our capitals, our commerce, our life as a whole
are still British to the core. If we only be true to our ideals of righteousness
and religion, if our patriotism continue moral and sincere, we shall have the
power to absorb the foreign elements that throng to us in commerce, and
stamp them with our own spirit (G.A. Smith 1903: 105).

Smith reacts against those commentators who, after Rudyard Kipling's
use of Nahum at the Jubilee of Queen Victoria as a warning call to the
British Empire, interpreted Assyria's fall as a wake-up call to Britain.
Cleland (1956: 957-58) sees the connection, too, though concurs with
Kipling's menacing comparison of Britain to Assyria.

Smith's discussion bolsters Said's contention that the construction of
the Orient serves the purposes of the empires of Europe: the author,
apparently without any self-consciousness, views the ancient and contemporary scenes before him through the lens of his supreme confidence in the moral and physical might of the British Empire. Given his
own commercial interests, it is little wonder that the patriot Smith would
caution against bloody overthrow of the oppressor and see patient waiting on the administration of law as the 'proper' response to a perceived
injustice. And it is little wonder that he never entertains the possibility
that the call for the demolition of an empire might be the word of God
rather than the hot-headed complaint of an Oriental mind.

Just as clearly, the quote from Smith also demonstrates how unsuccessful he is in distancing himself from the very faults he finds in the
Orient. The Nahum whom Smith lambastes for not extending God's
concern universally to all nations finds its echo, and not its antithesis, in
the twentieth-century commentator who calls his compatriots to keep
Britain pure from the foreigners on whom its defense depends.

ii. *Prophets do not call for revenge; poets do.* The conclusion of these
commentators that Nahum is a nationalistic poet rather than a prophet
relies both on the (ironic) denigration of nationalism and on the definition of a 'true', 'ethical' prophet as one who calls for the punishment
of his own people.

None of these writers explains why the call for the brutal destruction
of one's own people is morally superior to the call for the brutal
destruction of the enemy or the call for brutal destruction of them both.
J.M.P. Smith's (1911) preference for Jeremiah over Nahum, for example,
focuses only on Jeremiah's laments while ignoring Jeremiah's insistence
that Judah must be punished:

> And in this place I will make void the plans of Judah and Jerusalem, and
> will make them fall by the sword before their enemies, and by the hand of
> those who seek their life. I will give their dead bodies for food to the birds
> of the air and to the wild animals of the earth (Jer. 19.7).

> Who will have pity on you, O Jerusalem, or who will bemoan you? Who
> will turn aside to ask about your welfare? (Jer. 15.5).

The claim that Jeremiah takes no delight in imagining the downfall of the
enemy, as the ICC asserts, similarly ignores the Oracles against the
Nations in Jeremiah 46–51.

The distinction between 'prophet' and 'poet' made by these interpreters is a problematic one for several reasons. First, such a distinction
ignores the literary nature of the other prophetic literature, the way in
which the books are crafted in order to create the impressions they do—
for example, how the literary style of Jeremiah's confessions invites a
reader to distinguish between the compassionate Jeremiah and the harsh
word he was compelled to deliver.

Second, to demote Nahum from prophet to poet implies that the book
itself is thereby contained and controlled. The nationalism of Nahum is
allowed to disqualify it as divine word (though, as I suggested above, the
nationalism of interpreters is not allowed to render *their* theological
judgments invalid); if Nahum is 'merely' art, the interpreter can pass
judgment on it rather than be challenged by its theological claims. Such
an understanding, as I shall explore later in this chapter, underestimates
the interplay of the aesthetic and the violent in Nahum, the sheer power
(and, ultimately, the destabilizing effect) of its persistent ability to please
the very commentators who find its claims most offensive.

B. Response 2: Historical Contextualization

While the move to distance oneself from the violence of Nahum is still
prevalent in current interpretation (including the feminist interpreters I
discussed in the last chapter), the dominant trend since the second half
of the twentieth century has been toward a more empathetic understanding of the book. By emphasizing the historical context of the
book—the brutality of Assyrian oppression and the resultant suffering of
ancient Judah—this reading strategy attempts to exonerate or at least
explain the book's vehemence.

To demonize Assyria is not a difficult task. The Assyrians come across
as cruel, barbaric colonizers not only in the biblical material but even
more so in the documents and palace reliefs crafted by the Assyrians
themselves. Ashurbanipal's boasts of the multitude of enemies that were
slain, as well as the well-published reliefs of the siege of Lachish, help
shape the image of the brutal Assyrians. (See Introduction for further
details, and consult Plates 2-5.)

1. *Understandable rage*. But while the Assyrian materials have been
known since the early decades of the twentieth century, only late in the

century did that knowledge lead to a more sympathetic reading of Nahum. Consider, for example, the difference between Cleland in the *IB* of the 1950s (quotation above), who spoke of Jesus as the answer to Nahum, and Francisco García-Treto in the *NIB* of the 1990s, who offers a historical contextualization of the book's joy over the defeat of Assyria. After reviewing the Late Assyrian Empire, replete with a chart of Late Assyrian kings, García-Treto (1996: 595) concludes:

> It is easy to see how a Judean consciousness, formed by well over one hundred years of Assyrian hegemony and buttressed by brutal militarism and propaganda, could react with elation at the news of Assyria's collapse. The Judahites perceived that Yahweh had accomplished Nineveh's down-fall. What could be more natural than to cast the defeat of a long-hated oppressor as the long-sought after deliverance finally granted by a 'jealous and avenging God'?

In a similar way, Peter Craigie (1985: 58) underscores the brutality of the Assyrian menace:

> In order to understand its force and power, one must first attempt to enter Nahum's world… Assyria claims a place of pre-eminence among evil nations…it embarked upon a path of imperial expansion which knew no limitations of human decency and kindness.

In these and related treatments, Nahum becomes a more understandable and sympathetic voice. According to Craigie (1985: 59), Nahum is not a patriot or a nationalist but the voice of pent-up rage and oppression: 'If, from the comfort of study or pew, we complain that the sentiments of this book are neither noble nor uplifting, we need to remind ourselves that we have not suffered at Assyrian hands.'

From such a vantage point, Nahum becomes more akin to the 'ethical' prophets. Van der Woude (1977), who argues that Nahum was written in Assyria itself, among those exiled during the fall of Samaria, sees Nahum fulfilling a mission analogous to that of the 'hope-inspiring' prophets: 'If he lived in Assyria, was his situation not essentially the same as Ezekiel's and Deutero-Isaiah's in Babylon?' (1977: 136). In these treatments, Nahum's relief over the fall of a hated oppressor is understandable, even ethical.

2. *Resistance Literature.* The historical contextualization of Nahum has taken a distinctively liberationist turn in the work of Willie Wessels, whose 1998 'Nahum: An Uneasy Expression of God's Power' identifies Nahum as 'resistance literature', the voice of the oppressed against tyranny. According to Wessels, Nahum shares important features with the protest poetry of the anti-apartheid movements in South Africa. Both

sets of poetry challenge the dominant hegemonic system by construing an alternative ideological world: Nahum, by imagining the fall of Judah's oppressor, granted hope to a Judah under the thumb of the Assyrians. In this alternative world-making, literary style becomes integral and not incidental to political action: the emotive power of Nahum's language, the 'coarseness' that offended Calkins and the blood that stains the pages of the book function to shock and alter consciousness. According to Wessels (1998: 625):

> The call on the imagination of the people of Judah to picture the bloody defeat of the people of Nineveh should not be taken literally. It is not so much a call to violence or a legitimation of violence, but a call on the imagination of the people to picture the defeat of their enemy at the hands of a sovereign power, the power of Yahweh… If fear of the Assyrians with their strongholds and weaponry can be replaced by trust in the ability of Yahweh, it will change the future of the people of Judah.

According to Wessels, Nahum calls not for physical resistance to the Assyrians but rather for the ideological resistance to Assyria's apparent control over world affairs.

Comparisons between Nahum and anti-apartheid poetry suggest the fruitfulness of Wessels's suggestion; the two are easily read as variations of a genre. The works included in Barry Feinberg's collection, *Poets to the People: South African Freedom Poems*, forcefully express anger and the desire for revenge. A.N.C. Kumalo's 'Red our Colour' (Feinberg 1980: 58) demands 'Let's have poems blood-red in colour/Poems that tear at the oppressor's face'. amd in 'If Poets Must Have Flags', David Evans (Feinberg 1980: 20-21) underscores the role of poetry in resistance to the critics who ask poets 'to fugue human cries of pain', Evans replies, 'if we must have flags let them always be red'.

Both Nahum and these South African writers envision the poet as the one who enflames emotion for the sake of the struggle against the oppressor.

Like Nahum, Evans exhumes the corpses, sings the brave deeds of war, and wraps round its banner the guts of the dead. Along with resistance poetry from other parts of the globe, these works intertwine the aesthetic and the political. According to Harlow (1987: 28-29, 85):

> Resistance literature calls attention to itself, and to literature in general, as a political and politicized activity. The literature of resistance sees itself furthermore as immediately and directly involved in a struggle against ascendant or dominant forms of ideological and cultural production… resistance poetry challenge[s] dominant and hegemonic discourse of an occupying or colonizing power by attacking the symbolic foundations of that power and erecting symbolic structures of its own.

Nahum challenges the ideological hegemony of Assyria through the power of its art; and thus its ability to evoke the sense of immediacy and bloody detail (seen by many commentators as evidence of its author's chronological proximity to the events he describes) serves a political purpose.

The invocation of the image of the Divine Warrior (both in the opening theophany and in the battle scene of ch. 2) serves a political purpose as well. In much the same way as Burlein (2002) describes the history-telling of the racist Right as authorizing a way of remembering the past that challenges the dominant culture, so too the memory of a Divine Warrior who crushes all opponents stands as a 'counter-memory' to the historical record of pan-Assyrian conquest. As Aberbach highlights (1993: 8), the poetry of the prophets is replete with the imagery of iron, the very technology that enabled Assyrian hegemony: 'The poetry of the prophets echoes with iron: soldiers on the march, horses galloping, the glint of javelins, the thrust of swords, the clang of chariots.' In a defiant act of counter-memory, Nahum places iron not in the hands of the oppressor but in the hands of Yahweh, whose armies overwhelm Nineveh (p^{e}lādâ, Nah. 2.4).

The link that Wessels makes between Nahum and contemporary resistance poetry is helpful and important. Unlike earlier commentators who struggle to reconcile Nahum's violence with its literary skill, his proposal integrates the two by demonstrating how the boldness of the art serves the purposes of political defiance. Moreover, Wessels brings to the reading of Nahum post-colonialist sensibilities, highlighting and challenging the privilege from which the book's detractors have read.

Indeed, while to my knowledge Wessels is the only interpreter to link Nahum explicitly with resistance literature, his insistence that Nahum is most fairly understood as the voice of the oppressed is shared by many late twentieth-century commentators. Craigie (1985: 59) makes this point explicitly in a statement partially quoted earlier:

> The passions and feelings given vent in the Book of Nahum are those of a man and a nation who have suffered terror and oppression. And if, from the comfort of study or pew, we complain that the sentiments of this book are neither noble nor uplifting, we need to remind ourselves that we have not suffered at Assyrian hands.

Craigie's sensibilities are less explicitly post-colonialist than those of Wessels. While he is accurate that no contemporary reader has experienced Assyrian oppression, in a global context the 'we' of 'we have not suffered' does not apply to all persons. Nonetheless, like Wessels, Craigie stresses that oppression itself is an evil, one against which the voice of the subaltern must be heard and validated. His comments are quite different from those of H. Saggs (1965: 188; quoted in Aberbach 1993: 8), who claimed that Assyrian oppression was a boon to Judaism (and Christianity):

> Imperialism is not necessarily wrong: there are circumstances in which it may be both morally right and necessary. Such was the case in the Near East in the early first millennium. But for the Assyrian Empire the whole of the achievements of the previous 2000 years might have been lost in anarchy, as a host of tiny kingdoms (like Israel, Judah and Moab) played at war amongst themselves, or it might have been swamped under hordes of the savage peoples who were constantly attempting to push south-wards from beyond the Caucasus.

Surprisingly (at least to me), the positive assessment of Assyrian hegemony is shared by Aberbach as late as 1993 (8):

> Assyrian imperialism forced upon Judah the discipline of monotheism and its teachers, the prophets. If left alone, Judah might have abandoned its faith and submitted to the paganism which dominated the Near East, making it far more vulnerable to assimilation and disappearance.

According to Aberbach, the Assyrians are to be credited for Jewish survival. Small nations cannot be trusted to settle their own affairs.

Aberbach is almost alone among late twentieth-century commentators in extolling the virtues of Assyrian hegemony. As the examples of Wessels and Craigie indicate, the trend is much more toward a sympathetic reading of a book that speaks from the margins. Craigie (1985: 58) carries this effort further, by accentuating Assyrian brutality:

> Just as Nazi Germany still evokes the images of terror in the minds of those Jewish people who survived the Holocaust, so too in Nahum's world Assyria was the embodiment of human evil and terror.

By correlating Assyrian rule with the Holocaust, Craigie not only evokes an Other that has come to epitomize evil but he also implicitly challenges the anti-Judaism of an earlier age: the vengefulness that G.A. Smith (1903) in *The Expositor's Bible* could denigrate as 'Jewish nationalism' is affirmed by Craigie as the appropriate response to Ultimate Evil. Nahum becomes the voice of the Warsaw Ghetto.

Clearly, this insistence on reading Nahum as the response of an oppressed people challenges those commentators who arrogantly view themselves as superior to this violent book. Nahum's judgment of Assyria also holds as judgment against the Western, privileged orientation of commentaries such as that *The Expositor's Bible*, which itself recognized that the British Empire finds its analogue in Assyria and not in Judah.

For all its post-colonialist and liberationist appeal, the attempt to explain, account for, or vindicate Nahum via historical contextualization, including its identification with resistance literature, remains problematic. First and foremost, such a reading of the book depends on dating—and leaving—the book in the Assyrian period. Judah must be oppressed and Assyria must be a real and present threat for the rhetoric to function as resistance literature, for it to 'challenge dominant and hegemonic discourse of an occupying or colonizing power' (Harlow 1987: 85). Assyria must be a Nazi-like, pandemic, *and present* Evil against which resistance is morally incumbent.

In the Introduction, I discussed various reasons why the dating of Nahum to the Assyrian period is not certain. Even those who posit an Assyrian core to the book acknowledge that Nahum, both alone and possibly in relation to other prophetic books, was edited and given its final shape later than the Assyrian period.

But even should historical contextualization explain the original impetus for the book of Nahum, it does not account for the way in which the book functions for any reader after the seventh century BCE. Reading over the shoulder of a seventh-century audience, readers of later generations would *either* have to generalize any reference to Assyria (substitute 'Assyria' with the oppressor of your choice) *or* create a mental image of the 'historical' Assyria, trying to read Nahum as its first readers might have done, trying to share their moral outrage. An easy historical location of Nahum in the period of Assyrian brutality neither takes seriously the historical period of the book's formation nor the rhetorical strategies by which the book creates an image of Assyria for the reader via direct description and via (intentional?) intertexts. History alone cannot explain Nahum's references to Assyria.

Similarly, a generalized history of the Assyrians ('they were brutal oppressors') cannot explain the rhetorical function that Assyria plays in Nahum. While, as Wessels points out, poetry that rails against an oppressor can indeed galvanize resistance, such rhetoric can function in other ways as well. Rowlett's treatment of the language of Joshua argues that threats of the annihilation of the enemy can function as internal control: 'a pious-sounding rhetoric of divine control is employed in the service of a hierarchy that is simultaneously political and religious' (Rowlett 1996: 111). That is, language *explicitly* addressed to outsiders who threaten a community is *implicitly* a challenge to those within the community itself. Floyd (2000: 64) suggests the same for Nahum:

> By fictively addressing the Ninevehites in this vein, this speech informs the Judahite audience that their God is in control of the present international situation even though the imperial powers do not recognize him. It presents to its Judahite audience the negative example of a nation that inadvertently [!] finds itself in opposition to Yahweh, because it did not

learn from its own historical experience the lesson of its limitation (my
exclamation mark).

Though labeled a *maśśā'* against Nineveh, Nahum was read not by
Ninevites but by Judahites, and its promise that God will exact vengeance against his enemies holds for Judahites as well.

Scott's (1990) study of the 'arts of resistance' explores the rhetorical
elasticity of the language of power and demonstrates the difficulty in
discerning the intention behind a given public action. A public act of
deference can arise from ritual or routinized behavior, or it may disguise
a subversive 'hidden transcript'. While Scott focuses on non-public
defiance, his observation holds true for open resistance as well.

An anecdotal example from my own teaching experience highlights
how the 'same' language can mean different things. A student, who came
to my institution in the United States after spending time in South
African jails for his anti-apartheid activities, explained to me that South
African parties with diverse aims often used the same language: 'When
some people said "Death to the Boer"', Thulani told me, 'they were
calling for the deaths of all white South Africans. But when others said
the same thing, they meant "Death to the system" and were not
condoning violence.'

Reconstructing the complex way in which Nahum's rhetoric resonated
with and against the political realities of the seventh century BCE requires
a unattainable depth of understanding of ancient culture. If language
both reveals and masks resistance; if Nahum's rhetoric threatened Judahites as well as the ideological hegemony of Assyria; if, as Scott contends,
the invisibility of resistance serves the interest of the subordinate—then
drawing any particular correlation between the words of a heavily
redacted prophetic book and its effect on the politics of a particular time
period is a more complex undertaking than Wessels and others suggest.

C. Response 3: It is Not about Violence; it is about God

While the two previous responses to Nahum—both that of rejection and
that of historical contextualization—differ markedly in their appreciation
of the book, both assume a straightforward interpretation of its violence:
Nahum calls for, or at least imagines, human revenge against the
Assyrians. A third response suggests otherwise, interpreting Nahum as a
theological affirmation of the sovereignty and justice of God. By positing
Yahweh as the ultimate Warrior who defeats all enemies, Nahum does
not advocate active resistance by its readers but rather it seeks to
convince them of the power of God.

Elizabeth Achtemeier (1986: 5-6) draws such a distinction between
divine and human activity:

> Nahum is not primarily a book about human beings, however—not about
> human vengeance and hatred and military conquest—but a book about
> God. And it has been our failure to let Nahum be a book about God that
> has distorted the value of this prophecy in our eyes.

In a nearly identical sentence, Christensen (1988: 736) maintains:
'Nahum is primarily a book about God's justice, not about human vengeance, hatred, and military conquest.'

Such an understanding is often promoted by those who believe that
the opening theophany is a redactional addition to the book. For
example, Herbert Marks (1987: 216-17) explains:

> Readers who value the austere emphasis on cultic purity and social justice
> in Amos, Hosea, and Micah have thus tended to depreciate a prophet who
> seems content to glorify vengeance. Yet it is precisely here that we must
> distinguish between the early strata of the book and the final setting; for in
> the edited collection, the reader comes to Nahum's vision of martial
> triumph by way of an independent hymnic composition, celebrating God's
> supernatural power, and presenting his ultimate control of historical ends
> as an aspect of his primal authority over all creation... In this context, the
> destruction of Nineveh is no longer an aggressive vindication of Jewish
> nationalism, but, more generally, an illustration of God's universal govern-
> ment. As in Obadiah, a specific prophecy may now be read either with
> reference to its historical setting or within a revisionary frame that tends
> toward eschatology.

Similarly, Rex Mason (1991: 82) argues that the final redactional frame of
the book makes Nineveh a symbolic enemy:

> It is to be noted that the 'enemy' is not just a national one. Nineveh, as it is
> treated in the final form of the book, stands for all that is opposed to God
> and is characterized by false religion and inhuman oppression and cruelty.

That is, for Mason and Marks, while the original kernel of the book
may have vented its spleen against Assyria, the book as it stands makes a
larger point about God's sovereignty. Within its current redactional
frame, the fall of Nineveh becomes but one example of God's ultimate
power over his enemies.

A consistent theme among these interpreters who stress the theological message of Nahum is that God *must* avenge wrongdoing in order
to be a just God. For example, Achtemeier follows her quote (which I
cited above) regarding the distinction between divine and human
vengeance with the insistence on the necessity of God's punishing evil
(1986: 10):

> For if God does not destroy the evil human beings have brought into God's
> good creation, the world can never return to the wholeness he intended
> for it in the beginning. To divest God of his function as destroyer of wrong

is to acquiesce to the present corrupt state of the world—to accept the sinful status quo and simply to put up with whatever is done by selfish and prideful and corrupted men and women... Notably, however, Nahum emphasizes that God will be the destroyer of wrong and corruption.

In a quote that I discussed earlier in 'Nahum and Women', Peels (1995: 278) shares Achtemeier's perspective and argues that vengeance restores God's honor:

If it is said of this God, who is King, that He avenges himself, this can no longer be considered to be indicative of an evil humour, a tyrannical capriciousness, or an eruption of rancour. God's vengeance is kingly vengeance. If He takes vengeance, He does so as the highest authority exercising punishing justice. The vengeance of God is the action of God-as-King in the realization of his sovereign rule. This action is directed against those who offend God's majesty through transgression against his honour, his justice or his people.

And Mason (1991: 83) follows suit:

Any declaration of faith that the ultimate purpose of God for his world is a moral one cannot be wholly superficial or misguided... Taken together, the two books [Nahum and Jonah] say that in both judgment and mercy God is working out his purposes of justice and order in his world. Whatever appearances to the contrary there may be at times, in this world the last word will be, not with the apparently invincible powers of evil, but with God.

While the commentators mentioned so far in this chapter speak within Christian contexts, the positive evaluation of divine anger against injustice is most powerfully made by a Jewish interpreter. In his magisterial volume on the prophets, Abraham Joshua Heschel discusses the theological necessity of divine pathos. Heschel's God is not the impassive deity of the Platonists but rather the agonizing God whose anger burns against wrong (1962: 284):

The message of wrath is frightful indeed. But for those who have been driven to the brink of despair by the sight of what malice and ruthlessness can do, comfort will be found in the thought that evil is not the end, that evil is never the climax of history.

Commentators such as Heschel respond with comfort and not disgust to Nahum's threefold refrain:

A God jealous and vengeful is Yahweh;
vengeful is Yahweh and a master of anger;
vengeful is Yahweh to this enemies and he rages against his enemies
(Nah. 1.2).

Only a God who cares about what happens in the world gets angry—and acts to restore justice.

On the one hand, the commentators who stress that Nahum speaks of divine rather than human anger offer several important correctives to other treatments of Nahum. First, they take into account the final form of the book. Unlike the historical contextualization approach which places primary importance on the seventh-century context of Nahum's original kernel, those who stress the book's theological affirmation recognize that its opening theophany does not mention Nineveh and that, in the course of speaking of the enemy, it makes distinctive claims about the character of Judah's deity. Second, these commentators challenge a sentimental notion of forgivingness. Like those who read Nahum alongside resistance literature, they take injustice seriously; they recognize the danger of passivity in the face of evil and the political interests that are served by a God who does *not* act to thwart the powerful. Additionally the Christians among them challenge a notion long ago deemed heresy by the Church—that the Old Testament's God of wrath is inferior to the New Testament's God of love.

On the other hand, the attempt to distance Nahum from human violence by stressing its theological message ignores several important interpretative issues. Clearly, this approach assumes that the reader identifies with God—seeing the world, seeing Nineveh, as God sees. More accurately, this approach assumes that the reader accepts the book's depiction of God's feelings and emotions.

In several ways, Nahum complicates the reader's identification with the divine perspective. As I explored in the chapter 'Nahum and Women', both the personification of Nineveh as a woman and the portrayal of the city's fall as a rape invite or lead women readers (and those who read with women) to see themselves standing not with God but as or with the victim. Similarly, as I discussed in the commentary, Nahum's ever-shifting pronouns keep the reader off guard, precluding any permanent sense of the ones against whom the book's (God's) anger is directed.

In stressing the righteousness of God's indignation, these commentators also downplay—or outright ignore—the type of punishment Nahum envisions and the glee with which it is narrated. Their gaze remains fixed on the opening theophany of Nahum and the way in which it literally frames Nahum to be a book about God. The graphic violence of Nahum 3 receives far less attention. In a sobering reminder that not all women read as or with the raped one, Achtemeier's exposition of Nah. 3.1-7 (1986: 24) assumes the validity of Nahum's perspective. Without protest, she summarizes the message of Nahum 3:

> Indeed, finally the harlot will be done to death… But there are no mourn-
> ers who will be at her grave, and there are none to comfort her in the
> present as she sees her doom rise up to meet her.

While these readings make the case for the theological value of God's
anger, they do not address Nahum's *Schadenfreude*. While Portmann
argues that *Schadenfreude*—the pleasure at someone else's misfor-
tune—can have an ethical component ('When it springs from an abhor-
rence of evil or injustice, *Schadenfreude* might even be considered
exemplary'; Portmann 2000: 200), what distinguishes the savoring of
justice from the 'malicious glee' that Portmann deems unacceptable? The
commentators who focus on Nahum's theological claims do not address
such a question. Why, if the book is about justice, is the punishment that
is meted out on the woman's body given such detailed attention? Why
the taunts?

IV. The Limitations of These Responses

While both the identification of Nahum as resistance literature and the
positive evaluation of divine anger make contributions to the exploration
of the book's violence, I have suggested that both fall short as interpretative frameworks. Resistance literature leaves the 'true meaning' of
the book in the seventh century BCE, failing to account for its continued
effect on readers; and the limiting of Nahum to a theological treatise on
the sovereignty of God ignores the interplay between the book's
ideology and human political struggles. Neither response answers the
concerns of feminist commentators, explored in the previous chapter,
who object to the sexism and brutality with which the punishment of
Nineveh is depicted. Both responses explain Nahum as alternative-
world-building, as creating the ideological space for resistance and/or
the necessary fealty to the deity in whose hands Judah's destiny lies; but
neither comments on the nature of the ideological world thereby
created, particularly the perpetuation of the cycle of violence.

In her study of resistance literature, Harlow (1987) traces the 'dark
side' of resistance movements, how oppressed groups treat their own
causes as pristine and manifest little capacity for acknowledging their
own acts of oppression. She cites Maxime Rodinson's study of the Kurds
and Kurdistan, in which Rodinson laments:

> Ideology always goes for the simplest solutions… The slightest criticism is
> seen as criminal sacrilege. In particular, it becomes quite inconceivable
> that the oppressed might themselves be oppressing others. In an ideo-
> logical conception, such an admission would imply that the object of
> admiration was flawed and hence in some sense deserving of past or
> present oppression (Rodinson, cited in Harlow 1987: 29)

The tendency to reverse the tables, for the oppressed to fashion themselves after the image of their oppressors, is well documented in ancient
and contemporary resistance movements. In terms of biblical texts,
Fontaine (1997: 96) notes how many 'liberating' texts are themselves
problematic:

> Miriam's exultation in her war-god easily glosses over the fate of the
> Egyptians; Hannah's joy in her pregnancy expresses itself in the gleeful
> observation of the wicked getting their 'just desserts'; and this same theme
> dominates Mary's Magnificat.

And she plaintively asks (p. 97):

> Are the sentiments expressed, however human and understandable,
> actually sentiments we want to flourish and grow? Is the answer to the
> violence visited on women and children to mete out the same treatment to
> little boys and men?

In more recent historical memory, the 'turned tables' of Hutus and
Tutsis and Israelis and Palestinians highlight the same dynamics: when a
group sees itself as a perpetual victim, taking responsibility for its own
behavior toward other victims becomes difficult. Ellis (1997: 140-41),
commenting on how the perpetuation of Jewish victimhood has obscured
Palestinian suffering, maintains:

> If Jews have been abused in the Holocaust as innocent people and freeze
> that abuse as if it is happening today, then the question of Jewish cul-
> pability in the present can be deflected and rendered peripheral… The
> pretense to innocence leads to an insularity that not only shields Jews from
> accountability but also limits Jewish solidarity with others who are
> struggling and suffering.

The issue I raise is not simply to what extent Nahum exhibits a 'malicious' as opposed to 'ethical' *Schadenfreude* (in the terms that Portmann
describes), or what one should make of Wiesel's comment, 'God,
merciful God, do not have mercy on those who had no mercy on Jewish
children' (quoted in Ellis 1997: 172). Rather, my concern is directed
even more sharply at the attempt by commentators to 'solve' Nahum's
violence by linking it with resistance literature or stressing its vision of
God. Is Nahum less problematic in calling for rape and dismemberment
if its voice arises from the oppressed rather than the oppressor? Is the
book deemed more palatable if God rather than a human being rapes
and pillages?

Problematically, both approaches to vindicating Nahum (linking it
with resistance literature and labeling it a theological treatise) follow the
book's lead in keeping the Assyrians as faceless, monolithic 'Others'.
Nahum works hard to obscure the face of the enemy: the fall of the city

is described in the metaphor of the harlot who 'naturally' deserves the punishment she receives; the fallen of Nineveh are sexless bodies; and the reality that (innocent?) children will die in the march of the Divine Warrior is never addressed directly, but only inferred when Nineveh is compared to Thebes, whose children (also) were dashed to pieces at the head of every street. Following suit, commentators keep Assyrians faceless as well. Those whose bodies are strewn on Nineveh's streets become for commentators mere ciphers for 'oppressors' or 'evil' or 'enemies of God'. The distinctive characteristics of the Assyrians, as opposed to Babylonians or Persians or any other population group in the ancient world, are discussed only when the documentation of the Assyrian imperial regime can help generalize the Assyrians as 'ultimate evil'.

I contend that the problem of violence in Nahum is not only a problem of its explicit violence but also a problem of its ideological frameworks that undergird mentalities of violence. Nahum's rhetorical attempt to deny any connection between Self and Other and its portrait of Assyria as a monolithic evil empire find common cause with ancient and contemporary demonization of the Other for the purposes of annihilation. The more unsympathetic, faceless, and totally 'Other' the oppressor can be seen to be, the more easily its obliteration can be cheered—and less likely the oppressed will be able to acknowledge their own present or future complicity in atrocity.

As Burlein (2002: 201, 385) explains in her own response to those who demonize the racist Right:

> I am troubled by the stalemate that arises as both sides become mirror images: representing each other as 'Nazis' and 'extremists' with equal abandon; each fostering, feeding and even co-creating that which it seeks to oppose. What troubles me about this dynamic is not that it happens; what troubles me is how, from within, this stalemate feels like motion.

Labeling as evil either Nahum (along with turn-of-the-century Christian interpreters) or the Assyrians (along with those who speak of Nahum as resistance literature) feels, too, like a stalemate.

V. Another Response to Nahum

My own response to the violence of Nahum is grounded in two convictions that stand at apparent odds with one another. On the one hand, I find its ideological 'othering' and misogynistic rhetoric dangerous, too familiar to my own experience and the experience of others to be dismissed as 'just literature'. On the other hand, the connection of Nahum with resistance literature challenges my own hubris, as one who benefits from colonializing cultures, in passing judgment on what the oppressed should or should not say.

In what follows, I should like to work within the tension between these convictions. Clearly, this work must be carried out at the level of the book's rhetoric and ideological construction, for it is Nahum's world construction that does its work on the reader. Here, I explore what insights literary and ideological theory might shed on a response to Nahum.

A. The Other as Self

Psychoanalytic theory, particularly that of Jacques Lacan and Luce Irigaray, suggests that, as a project, Othering is a slippery business. Not only are the Other and the Self intricately intertwined, but also the oppositional differences on which the distinction between the two depend ultimately prove unstable.

As Beal (1997) discusses in his application of Irigaray to the book of Esther, the problem of the Other is always a problem of the Self. The construal of the Other is an attempt to shape one's own identity; the impulse toward self-definition arises from the anxiety of the Self. The Other becomes the site of what is abjected in the Self—that which the Self cannot or will not own. And yet, the apparent opposites are inseparably bound together, depending upon each other for their meaning. In Lacanian terms, the very one who lacks the phallus 'is' the phallus, the one with the paradoxical power to confirm the importance or non-importance of the phallus. Without the Other, the Self loses all points of reference.

Irigaray also argues that identity formation via oppositional difference cannot sustain itself. As Beal (1997: 68) characterizes her argument (along with that of Emmanuel Levinas):

> Otherness can be neither subsumed into sameness nor reduced to oppositional difference. Indeed, their work [Irigaray and Levinas] suggests a deep insecurity in the self that would project such visions of alterity, showing how the solidity of one's own identity depends precariously on the fixity of the other-as-object.

Identity, as Butler also argues, is built on too long a list of potentially contradictory requirements to remain fixed.

Such theory poses a question to the book of Nahum: What anxiety of Judah's identity drives Nahum's construction of Nineveh? Does, for example, the designation of Nineveh as a whore belie a question of Judah's own fidelity? Is that same anxiety raised when God briefly comments, 'I have oppressed you' without explaining *why*? Does Nahum really portray Judah as innocent (as commentators have suggested)? The concern with the king of Assyria's manliness—his ability to protect his female—likewise may suggest (as we saw in the previous chapter) an underlying question of Yahweh's ability to protect his own. When read in light of Lacan, the sheer energy that the book devotes to contrasting the weakness of Assyria with the overwhelming might of Yahweh suggests the paradoxical power of Assyria to confirm—or not to confirm—Yahweh's might. If Yahweh *has* the phallus, Assyria *is* the phallus.

Deconstruction joins with psychoanalytic theory in calling attention to Nahum's inability to sustain the oppositional differences on which the identities of Nineveh and Judah depend. As I have suggested throughout the commentary, the differences between 'us' and 'them' do not hold steady throughout the book. Pronouns without antecedents render difficult a simple identification of God's friend and God's enemy; and Nineveh's invitation to compare herself with Thebes spawns a web of identification among the feminine characters of the book that destabilizes the abjection of Nineveh.

But just as Nahum itself cannot ultimately 'Other' Nineveh, so too commentators cannot clearly demarcate the oppressed and oppressor. If Judah's fidelity and Yahweh's power are implicitly questioned, in what sense does Nahum assert divine vindication of the downtrodden? Recognizing the ambiguities and anxieties of Nahum's rhetoric moves the interpreter beyond the stalemate of choosing sides—having to choose to read with or against the oppressed.

B. Giving Faces to the Other

The epiphany of the face is ethical (Levinas 1961: 199).

If the fundamental ethical problem of Nahum is Othering-for-the-Sake-of-Annihilation, then strategies that challenge Othering serve in the formulation of a contrary response. The first strategy, as I have just explored, builds upon the recognition that Othering is a crisis of self-representation. A second strategy is to give faces to the Others whose identity Nahum attempts to obscure. While such a reading strategy could constitute pure counter-reading—the conscious attempt to read against the intentions of an author, to subvert a text's ideological aims by identifying with the 'wrong' character—in the case of Nahum the book's own rhetorical choices invite a reader to glimpse a human Assyrian face.

The casting of Nineveh as a whore serves as an example of how language's 'surplus of meaning' destabilizes ideological intent. On the one hand, by calling Nineveh a whore, Nahum effects a powerful Othering. Nineveh is not only Woman but Bad Woman, deserving whatever punishment she receives, with no one to sympathize with her plight. And yet, on the other hand, the feminization of Nineveh spawns (unintended?) reading consequences. By giving the enemy the face of a woman, who is further described as beautiful, Nahum opens itself to the diverse responses that readers have to women, and especially to women punished for their sexual transgressions. For feminist commentators, the feminization of Nineveh both invites resistance to the book and, ironically, allows the very means for that resistance: it is because Nahum has chosen the feminine face of Nineveh that feminists are able to identify with the book's intended foe. By feminizing Nineveh, Nahum allows feminist readers to put a face on the enemy; in the face of Nineveh, feminists can see their own faces, as well as those of Bosnian rape victims. No longer the abject Other, the foe becomes Victim-Like-Me.

The Other takes on a face in further ways in Nahum as well. Through its powerful portrayal of the realities of war—that 'immediacy' that its literary admirers praise—Nahum opens itself to being read intertextually with testimonies of war. The literature, and even more so the images, of contemporary bloody conflict give faces to the enemy of Nahum.

- Nahum 3.3 intertwines in the modern imagination with the well-disseminated images of the Shoah (see Plates 6 and 7), giving place and name and body shape to Nahum's breathless 'piles of dead, heaps of corpses, dead bodies without end—they stumble over the bodies!'
- Nahum 3.6 ('I will treat you with contempt and will set you as a sight') finds it twentieth-century intertext in the Poland of the 1940s (see Plate 8).
- And when Nah. 3.10 mentions the children ('even her infants were dashed in pieces at the head of every street'), there is no dearth of faces that haunt my reading—faces of Jewish children in the Shoah (see Plate 9); faces of children personalizing the mass grave at Cana, Lebanon (see Plate 10); faces of children around the world (see Plate 11). When Nahum takes on the cruelty of the Assyrians as his own, I see the faces of Hutus and Tutsis, Israelis and Palestinians, superimposed, one on the other. Presenting itself as a picture of war, whether real or imagined, Nahum joins the ranks with other pictures of war. And the pictures from the wars of my world have faces.

'Shattered is Nineveh. Who will mourn her?' The question for me is not a rhetorical one. I will. I will mourn those who die, locked together in war.

> I see these images of children burning
> This time they are not our own
> Or are they
> Burning everywhere (J. Moore, quoted in Ellis 1997: 38)

C. Fickle Pleasure

The comparison of Nahum to war photography is not merely evocative, but indeed returns us to the whole issue of the aesthetic in the book of Nahum. As I outlined above in my discussion of those who see Nahum as a nationalist poet rather than as a prophet, even those commentators who most denigrate the book praise its ability to create the image of war in the mind of the reader. They admit, too, that Nahum is aesthetically pleasing but thereby leave Nahum a tension of two contrary character-istics—its ethical inferiority and its literary artfulness.

Mining this apparent tension between Nahum's ethics and its art, however, opens another avenue into a discussion of its violence. Is the pleasure of reading Nahum quite so simple?

In their masterful study of Assyrian palace reliefs, Bersani and Dutoit (1985) explore the dynamics of aesthetic representation of Assyrian violence. They suggest ways in which the artistic style of the reliefs disrupts a straight reading of their accounts of military success. The artists' use of repeated forms, the play of curve and line, the incongruous details (e.g. a lion whose haunches—through varying depths of relief—are both inside and outside of a cage) not only engage the eye but also take attention away from the story being narrated: 'The force of this violent subject is, then, contravened by visual abstractions which disrupt the spectator's reading of the subject' (Bersoni and Dutoit 1985: 9) (see Plate 5).

Assyrian reliefs, Bersani and Dutoit suggest (1985: 9), exhibit 'extra-ordinarily ingenious strategies for diverting our attention from the stories':

> It is as if the subject of the hunt provided the artists of ancient Assyria with an exciting opportunity to experiment with unusual and dramatic formal arrangements… The sculptor can indulge in an extravagant play and ten-sion of lines, shapes, and directions without transgressing the limits of realistic representation (p. 35).

Given the aesthetic form in which it is narrated, how does the violence of Assyrian relief move its audience? Bersani and Dutoit suggest a multi-plicity of possible responses: (1) appreciating the art may minimize or delay the effects of the violent content; (2) the viewer may enjoy the violence, sadomasochistically; or, as Bersani and Dutoit underscore (3) the movement of the limbs, the play of the line, may 'cue a nonmimetic response' (1985: 37), keep us reading, viewing, searching.

Might the aesthetics of Nahum function in the third way Bersani and Dutoit suggest, performing a similar destabilizing function on its violent content? Perhaps Nahum's assonance, alliteration, metaphor (all the formal features that turn commentators' heads) not only attempt to 'sell' but also draw attention away from its violence. The following statement of Aberbach (quoted in Preminger and Greenstein 1986: 505-506) suggests such a reading:

> It [Nahum] is a poem of bloodshed and horror, of vengeance and destruction, with little to relieve its savagery and violence; but it must be admired for the sheer power and force of its expression and for its awful, but brilliant imagery… Nahum's poem on this critical juncture in history is, for the most part, devoid of theological rationalization and includes no word of compassion for the vanquished… But precisely because the poem lacks an overt theological message it stands on its own as a human document and an artistic achievement.

A book that opens with a theophanic hymn and which strives to undergird the power of God over evil has no 'overt theological message'? At least for Aberbach, the 'artistic achievement' of the book, takes precedence over the book's ideological intent.

VI. Conclusion

Much like the patriarchy that is the fishbowl for the treatment of gender in the book, the ideological distinctions that Nahum draws between 'us' and 'them' are the fishbowl of its violence. The two ideologies—patriarchy and Othering—are not independent of one another; they are articulated (in the sense of 'connected together') in a complex web of difference and division. Only by addressing those mentalities is there any possibility of a response to Nahum.

Addressing Nahum on the level of its ideology, I believe, avoids the pitfalls of both an easy 'No' to this book and an easy (or, for Wessels, an 'uneasy') 'Yes'. I accept the post-colonialist critique that Wessels's perspective offers; I cannot say 'No' to Nahum without saying 'No' to the voices of the oppressed. But I cannot embrace this book, either, not without calling attention to the ways in which it—and its myriad ancient and contemporary equivalents—puts on the mask of the oppressor against which it rails.

I and the culture in which I live are implicated in and complicated by the Othering function of language and society that runs through the book of Nahum. But perhaps, as Butler suggests, there might be a way to take up the master's tools and use them subversively. As the quote from Camus with which I opened this chapter suggests, there might be a way to reduce the number of tortured children—and adults.

Nahum and the Nations

> In every text there are traces of that which has been excluded or repressed
> (Beal 1992a: 24).

I. Introduction

In its single-minded attention to announcing punishment on a nation
other than Israel or Judah, Nahum joins the ranks of prophetic materials
designated as Oracles against the Nations (OAN). In this chapter, I shall
read Nahum intertextually—first, with selected OAN and then, for
reasons that I shall outline, with the book of Lamentations.

In the Introduction, I explained that by 'intertextuality' I refer not to
the traditional attempt of redaction critics to map a diachronic relationship between texts but rather to the poststructuralist consideration of
how the juxtaposition of multiple texts spawns new readings. As
explored in the work of Julia Kristeva and Mikhail Bakhtin, intertextuality in this vein considers interrelationships between materials on the
level of text reception, considering how reading two texts together
destabilizes them both.

Two quotes characterize this type of intertextuality—the first, from
Danna Fewell (1992: 17):

> No text exists in a vacuum. All texts are embedded in a larger web of
> related texts, bounded only by human culture and language itself. Inter-
> textual reading is inevitable.

And the second from Peter Miscall (1992: 44):

> The relationship between two texts is equivocal. It includes, at the same
> time, both acceptance and rejection, recognition and denial, understand-
> ing and misunderstanding, and supporting and undermining. To recognize
> that a text is related to another text is both to affirm and to deny the earlier
> text as a source that has been superseded. The later text displaces its
> model.

I am interested in how reading Nahum alongside similar texts might
focus my attention both on its generic and on its distinctive features—as
well as on the instabilities in Nahum that such a reading might expose.

II. The OAN and *massā'* Genres

Scholars recognize no standard list of OAN texts. Isaiah 13–23, Jeremiah 46–51, Ezekiel 25–32, Amos 1.3–2.16, Nahum, and Obadiah are widely recognized to fit this category, though some have suggested that the OAN are ubiquitous in the prophetic materials, absent only from Hosea.

Despite various attempts to discern a specific literary form of the OAN, most scholars now agree that thematic rather than structural similarities link these materials. Their distinguishing characteristic is their announcement and/or envisioning of the destruction of a nation other than Judah or Israel at the hands of Yahweh, God of Israel. Most of the texts describe the reason for this destruction in general terms. Occasionally lambasted for their treatment of Israel and/or Judah, more often the nations are accused of non-specific pride. Indeed, Robert Carroll (1986: 756) suggests that many of the OAN 'transcended their origins in xenophobic curses against other nations to become statements of a theological nature against hubris of any form'. Often the nation's transgression is not specified at all, its destruction serving primarily as a manifestation of Yahweh's ultimate sovereignty. Historically minded interpreters suggest that the OAN had their origins in the rituals of warfare and likely served to shape Judean foreign policy by demonstrating the folly of alliance with the nations.

As I suggested in the commentary on Nah. 1.1, the set of OAN texts overlaps with that of *massā'* texts. Both types of materials manifest a sharp dichotomy between the deity's friends and his enemies, and *massā'* texts often pit Israel or Judah against the nations. The two are distinguishable, however, since not all *massā'* texts are OAN (as in the case of Malachi) and since the label OAN is usually reserved for extended diatribes against a foreign nation.

III. Nahum and the OAN

Nahum can be read fruitfully with all of the OAN. For example, Nahum follows the same general structure as Isaiah 13, which turns to destruction of the Other and to salvation for Jacob only after a general theophany; both Nahum and Isaiah also address a male antagonist (the king of Assyria for Nahum, and the Day Star for Isa. 14). Similarly, Nahum joins with Ezekiel 25–31 in painting scenes of battle and siege (Ezek. 26.8-14; Nah. 2 and 3), in expressing concern with those who gaze at the enemy city's humiliation (Ezek. 27.35; 28.17-19; Nah. 3.5-7), and in raising a mock lamentation over the city's fall (Ezek. 32.16; Nah. 3.1). Here, however, I focus on reading Nahum alongside Jeremiah and

Obadiah, intertexts that collude and collide in important ways with our text at hand.

A. Nahum and Jeremiah 46–51

According to Carroll (1986: 754), '46–51 contains some of the finest, as well as the most difficult, poetry in the book of Jeremiah'. Indeed, the inconsistencies within the chapters and their haphazard organization have led many scholars to posit a long, complex editing process behind the present form of the book. In keeping with my attention to the final form of biblical materials, I will focus not on the book's compositional history but rather the effects of its final presentation.

Widely recognized as a distinct section of the book of Jeremiah, chs. 46–51 present a series of oracles against Others. Attention moves from Egypt, to the Philistines, to Moab, to the Ammonites, to Edom, to Damascus, to Kedar and Hazor, and finally to Babylon. Though each oracle stands alone, recurrent themes and phrases run throughout them. These texts paint scenes of battle, threaten the nations with exile, and, importantly, stress that the fall of these countries is attributable directly to Yahweh's vengeance. Indeed, *nāqām*—vengeance—is a frequent theme of Jeremiah, appearing in Jer. 5.9, 29; 9.8; 11.20; 15.15; 20.10, 12; 46.10; 50.15, 28; and 51.6, 11, 36. Carroll (1986: 819) appropriately concludes that the twin themes of Jeremiah 50–51 are Babylon's defeat as punishment and the restoration of Israel.

1. *Collusion.* In the course of its attention to other nations, Jeremiah 46–51 shares many commonalities with the book of Nahum:

Shared Vocabulary and Phrases

Text	Jeremiah	Nahum
nāqām, vengeance	46.10; 50.15, 28; 51.6, 11, 36	1.2
leonine imagery	49.19-20; 50.17, 44; 51.38	2.12-13
water imagery	46.2; 50.42; 51.36, 42, 44, 55	1.8; 2.8
troops as locusts	46.23; 51.14	3.15
troops become women	48.41; 49.22, 24; 50.43; 51.30	3.13
chaos of war as drunkenness	48.26; 51.7, 39, 57	3.11
incurable wound of enemy	51.8	3.19
shepherds	49.7-22, 19; 50.6, 44	3.18
vanquished leaders asleep	51.39, 57	3.18
'make an end' (*'āśâ kālâ*)	46.28 (same root in 49.37)	1.8

Shared Themes

Text	Jeremiah	Nahum
destruction addresses the honor of the fallen	51.24, 49	2.3
salvation of Judah	46.27; 50.33-34; 51.5, 10, 24, 35, 36	1.12-13; 2.1, 3
march of the Divine Warrior	50.25; 51.14-17	1.2-8
Yahweh's weapons	50.25, 35-38	2.4-6
dead in the streets	50.36; 51.4	3.3
vision of the city in battle	46.22-24; 47.13	3.1-3; 2.4-11
threat of exile	46.19; 48.7, 11	2.8
others gaze on the city's shame	46.39; 47.13; 49.13, 17; 50.13, 23; 51.24, 37	3.5-7
references to Judah's own punishment	46.28	1.12

Similarities in Style

Text	Jeremiah	Nahum
address to the antagonist	48.11-17; 51.31	1.14; 2.14; 3.18-19
feminine personification of the city	46.19-24; 47.3; 48.2, 9, 18; 49.4, 13; 51	3.4-7
taunt of the fallen city	51.8-9	2.12-13; 3.16-19
call to mourn	48.1, 17; 49.3; 50.27; 51.8	3.1
imperatives addressed to armies	46.3-4, 9; 49.14, 28-29; 50.14, 26-27; 51.8, 11, 12; 46.9	2.2; 3.14-15

This list is by no means exhaustive, but the similarities between Jeremiah 46–51 and Nahum highlight the observation made by others that the OAN employ a standard set of stock phrases, themes, and rhetorical stances. A recognition of the generic character of Nahum reminds the interpreter that, despite the negative judgments this book often receives, Nahum stands fully within the classical prophetic tradition. It is no more nationalistic than the beloved Jeremiah, to which it is often negatively compared. Nor is Nahum more bloodthirsty than Jeremiah, as seen in the paradigmatic equation in Jer. 48.10 between doing Yahweh's work and wielding the sword in bloodshed.

Jeremiah 46–51 and Nahum collude to show a Yahweh concerned with his own honor and with that of Judah. The ultimate crime of nations is their pride, failing to recognize Yahweh's superiority over and ultimate control of their destinies, though the nations' crimes against Judah are also punished.

In addition, reading Nahum alongside Jeremiah highlights the

This gender alternation is especially evident in Jeremiah 48, where Moab is both male and female, even in a single verse (48.18).

A classic case of the slippery application of gender is found in the oracle against Edom in Jeremiah 49. As Jer. 49.7 opens, the subject to be punished is male: 'Esau is stripped bare, *his* hiding places uncovered.' A shift occurs in 49.13, where Bozrah becomes the focus of ridicule and pronouns shift to female: *she* now becomes the object of cursing, and Yahweh calls nations to gather against *her*. When in 49.17 attention returns to Edom, however, feminine pronouns do not disappear: 'Edom (masculine) shall become an object of horror; everyone who passes by her (feminine) will be horrified and will hiss because of all of her disasters.' Indeed, feminine pronouns are used for Edom throughout the oracle.

On the surface, this oracle of Jeremiah appears less gender-specific than does Nahum. It calls nations male as well as female and does not focus punishment on the female. Moreover, when Jeremiah *does* announce punishment of females, its language appears less explicitly sexualized than that of Nahum. Cities are called daughters, never whores, and while they are made into perpetual wastes and threshed like threshing floors, they are not sexually assaulted.

An intertextual reading of Jeremiah and Nahum complicates this simple picture—particularly a parallel reading of Nah. 3.4-7 and Jer. 49.8-13, both of which envision the physical exposure of the enemy:

Nah. 3.5-7	*Jer. 49.10*
I am against you, says Yahweh of hosts, and will lift up your skirts over your face; and I will let nations look on your nakedness and kingdoms on your shame. I will throw filth at you and treat you with contempt, and make you a spectacle. Then all who see you will shrink from you and say, 'Nineveh is devastated; who will bemoan her?' Where shall I seek comforters for you?	But as for me, I [Yahweh] have stripped Esau bare, I have uncovered his hiding places, and he is not able to conceal himself. His offspring are destroyed, his kinsfolk and his neighbors; and he is no more.

On its own, the stripping of the male Edom in Jer. 49.10 is a sign of humiliation and not overly sexual in nature; in contrast with that of Nineveh, Edom's nakedness is not made into a spectacle. When read intertextually with Nahum, however, Jeremiah's language takes on new nuances. The dual punishments of stripping and loss of offspring may be seen as not accidental but rather as causal. The sexual connotation of the exposure of the female bleeds over into the description of the exposure of the male, lending another nuance to vocabulary like 'his hiding places' or 'his private places'. Esau's punishment may be not only exposure, but also, like Nineveh's, sexual assault.

When Jer. 49.10 is read with sexual nuance, particular elements of verses that follow take on greater importance. In Jer. 49.18, the destruction of Edom is compared to the destruction of Sodom, which in Genesis 19 is the site of barely averted male–male sexual contact. To Sodomites who pound at his door wanting to lie with his male guests, Lot the sojourner offers his daughters instead. The rogues persist, and only the hand of the men of God can thwart the press of the men who wish to lie with other men. In Genesis, the prospect of men being ravished as women are ravished warrants divine intervention. Once read intertextually with Nahum, its sexual nuances exposed, Jer. 49.18 reads well alongside the Genesis account: 'As when Sodom and Gomorrah were overthrown, a man will not lie down there and a son of man will not sojourn in her.'

Jeremiah 49, when read alongside Nahum, raises the complications of male sexual assault. Jeremiah's alternation between male and female personification appears a deliberate strategy to avoid the possible sexual nuances of homoeroticism.

Nahum, when read alongside Jeremiah, becomes an even more patriarchal text. Jeremiah's ability to imagine the punishment of a male—even if to cringe before its implications—reminds the reader that Nahum's description of Nineveh's punishment as the sexual assault of a woman is not 'natural' but a deliberate rhetorical move. Similarly, the fact that Jeremiah can describe feminine cities as 'daughters' and avoid the explicit language of rape demonstrates that Nahum's language is not determined by its culture or by the larger prophetic tradition. Moreover, Jeremiah's latent concern with male–male sexual contact returns us to the observation raised in 'Nahum and (Wo)men' that the assault of Nineveh is a means of humiliating her male. Might Nahum, like Jeremiah, be avoiding any image of Yahweh's rape of a male character?

B. Nahum and Obadiah

The connections between Nahum and Jeremiah 49 invite a further intertextual linkage with the book of Obadiah. With minor variations, Obad. 1-5 duplicates Jer. 49.14-19, leading many scholars to consider them as identical texts. Obadiah is further linked with Nahum in that the two are the only book-length OAN in the Hebrew Bible.

Due to the overlap between Jeremiah 49 and Obadiah, many of my observations regarding Jeremiah pertain also to Obadiah. For example,

Nahum's sexualized language for assault spills over not only into Jer. 49.10 but also into Obad. 6: 'How Esau has been pillaged, his treasures searched out!' becomes less a complaint against the loss of material goods and more an image of personal humiliation.

More complicated effects are created by reading Nahum (and Jer. 49) alongside Obad. 10: 'For the slaughter and violence done to your brother Jacob, shame shall cover you, and you shall be cut off forever.' On the one hand, Obadiah colludes with Jeremiah 49 and Nahum in avoiding the sexual aspects of male exposure; here, Esau is not shamed by stripping but rather shame *covers* him. On the other hand, the male language of Obadiah and Jeremiah 49 collides with Nahum. Nahum's rhetoric depends on the recognition by the reader that Nineveh's stripping is justified because she is a whore. But Jeremiah and Obadiah not only suggest the elasticity of gender personification—how what is said about a man slides into what is said about a woman (and vice versa)—but also they imagine the stripping of one not called a whore. If exposure brings shame to men as well as to women and is used as punishment for those other than whores, then Nineveh's status as a whore fades as the justification for her treatment.

Other intertextual effects follow. Obadiah 10, like Nah. 2.2, suggests that Yahweh's actions are in response to the shaming of Jacob. Obadiah, however, indicates that honor is not Yahweh's only concern. In Obad. 19-21, unlike in Sodom and Gomorrah, something remains after everyone is destroyed—the land remains, to be taken by the exiles of the Israelites:

> Those of the Negeb shall possess Mount Esau, and those of the Shephelah the land of the Philistines; they shall possess the land of Ephraim and the land of Samaria, and Benjamin shall possess Gilead. The exiles of the Israelites who are in Halah shall possess Phoenicia as far as Zarephath; and the exiles of Jerusalem who are in Sepharad shall possess the towns of the Negeb. Those who have been saved shall go up to Mount Zion to rule Mount Esau; and the kingdom shall be Yahweh's.

In Obadiah, gain comes from the destruction of the enemy, and the same may be implied in Jer. 49.2, where Israel dispossesses those who dispossessed them. Does Nahum suggest similar interests? While Nahum makes no explicit mention of economic gain for Judah (Judah is called to celebrate her feasts, though they are not funded by loot from Nineveh), goods are the apparent concern behind the critique of the proliferation of Assyria's merchants in Nah. 3.16, and the reader is left to wonder if Yahweh alone enjoys the booty and plunder of Nah. 2.9.

Another complication that arises from the Jeremiah–Obadiah–Nahum intertextual triangle is explicitly ethical. Obadiah 12-13 admonishes Esau:

> But you [Esau] should not have gloated over your brother on the day of
> his misfortune; you should not have rejoiced over the people of Judah on
> the day of their ruin; you should not have boasted on the day of distress.
> You should not have entered the gate of my people on the day of their
> calamity; you should not have joined in the gloating over Judah's disaster
> on the day of his calamity; you should not have looted his goods on the
> day of his calamity.

Does the admonition hold for Jeremiah and Obadiah? Are they wrong to
gloat over their enemy's distress? And does Nahum, in imagining the
looting of the Divine Warrior's army (2.9) and in taunting the raped
Nineveh, undercut the ethical basis on which Obadiah accuses the
Other?

While intertextual possibilities offer infinite room for analysis, I mention but one additional effect of reading Nahum with its OAN intertexts:
the diminishing of Assyria's status as the uniquely and supremely evil
Other. Even from my short discussion here, it is clear that Nahum is not
alone in singling out an enemy for destruction. Obadiah devotes all its
energy to demonizing Edom, and the extended OAN series in Isaiah,
Jeremiah, and Ezekiel direct Yahweh's wrath against a wide array of
Israel's foes. As we have seen, much of the language used in these OAN
is generic and formulaic, employing stock phrases against the enemy at
hand. This simple observation alone complicates any attempt to mark a
nation as deserving of particular punishment. In the case of the verbal
overlap between Jeremiah and Obadiah, Jeremiah's efforts to portray
Edom as but one nation among many is destabilized by its verbal connection with Obadiah, which endeavors to convince its reader that
Edom's callousness is deserving of particular rage. Edom cannot be one
of many if it stands as paradigmatic; and Edom cannot be paradigmatic if
it is just one of many. When put into different frames, the 'same' accusations against Edom in Jeremiah and in Obadiah compete with rather
than support one another. Similarly, Nahum's connections with other
OAN remind its readers that other nations receive similar punishment
and that Yahweh the Divine Warrior also marches against Babylon,
Edom, and Moab. Nineveh may indeed be Other, but not uniquely so.

IV. Nahum and Lamentations

My choice to turn to the book of Lamentations as a final intertext to
Nahum is not an obvious one. Lamentations is not an OAN, not a
maśśā', not a prophetic book, not concerned with the Assyrians. More
often classified as a communal lament, Lamentations grieves the destruction of Jerusalem in 586 BCE by the Babylonian armies.

Much, however, holds these books together. Dobbs-Allsopp (1993), for example, argues that both Lamentations and the OAN manifest characteristics of the city lament, a genre whose presence in the Hebrew Bible he discerns from comparative Mesopotamian evidence. According to Dobbs-Allsopp, recurrent features of the city lament include the mourning over the destruction of a mighty city; the attribution of its fall to the gods; shifts in points of view; the contrast between the city's current fate and its glorious past; and detailed descriptions of infra-structure collapse and of the tragic fate of its people.

He briefly speculates that the strong correlation between the OAN and the city lament genre arises from the 'lament-to-invective movement' (1993: 161) common to the city laments: not only does lament over one's own city frequently turn to curse of the enemy but also the same entity can be both lamented and cursed (as seen in *The Curse of Agade*, see Cooper 1983).

It is precisely the correlation between lament of the Self and curse of the Other that draws me to an intertextual reading of Nahum with Lamentations. Both books envision a city's destruction, though from the standpoint of different characters. Nahum mockingly laments the fall of the Other, rejoicing over Nineveh's fate, while Lamentations mourns the Self, weeping over Jerusalem's desolation. I am interested in how deva-station is witnessed through the eyes of different characters—what looks the same and what looks different depending upon point of view, as well as how their convergence draws into focus yet another way of seeing.

A. Collusion

The commonalities between Lamentations and Nahum range from simple vocabulary to rhetorical strategies and ideology. On the level of vocabulary, Lam. 2.13 questions whether Jerusalem's 'break' (*šeber*) might be incurable, and Nah. 3.19 taunts the king of Assyria with the same: 'your wound (*šeber*) is incurable'. Both attribute to Yahweh anger (*'ap*, Nah. 1.6; Lam. 1.12; 2.1, 3, 21, 22; 3.43; 4.11), while yet affirming that he is 'good' (*tôb*, Lam. 3.25; Nah. 1.7); and both reveal that the fallen city has no comforters (verbal root *nāḥam*, Lam. 1.2, 9, 16, 17; 2.13; Nah. 3.7, the name 'Nahum').

In terms of style, both books describe the city's fall in progress. Just as Nahum describes advancing armies and the resultant chaos in chs. 2 and 3, so too Lamentations 2, 3, and 5 depict the present suffering of the inhabitants of Jerusalem. Both show the dead lying in the streets (Nah. 3.3; Lam. 2.21) and the body's response to anguish (Nah. 2.10; Lam. 2.11).

The books collude in personification as well. Both describe the destruction of the city as the humiliation of a woman. In Nahum the punishment is more sexually explicit than in Lamentations, but both utilize vocabulary that may bear sexual connotations: for example, 'she is exiled' (*gull^etâ* in Nah. 2.8 and *gāletâ* in Lam. 1.3) comes from the same verbal root as 'uncovered'. Others mock and gaze at the assaulted city (Lam. 2.15-16; Nah. 3.5-7).

Throughout both books, the agent of this humiliation is Yahweh the Divine Warrior (Lam. 2.3-8; Nah. 1.2-8), though neither offers specific reasons for the divine rage. As both Dobbs-Allsopp and Linafelt (2000) outline, Lamentations acknowledges but does not dwell on Jerusalem's guilt; her suffering receives far greater attention than her sinfulness. Similarly, Nahum provides little concrete information about Nineveh's crimes. Rather, her guilt is described metaphorically: she is a 'city of bloodshed, full of lies' (3.1), who 'enslaves nations through her debaucheries' (3.4). Only the enigmatic reference to the multiplication of her merchants (Nah. 3.16) suggests specific Assyrian crimes.

Ideologically, both Nahum and Lamentations draw a distinction between the Self and the Enemy. While in Lamentations Jerusalem attributes her destruction to Yahweh and acknowledges her own guilt, she still calls for her enemies to suffer as she has (1.21-22; 3.65-66; compare *The Curse of Agade*, line 212). Nahum does not report Nineveh's call for revenge, but throughout the book the city's fate is described as the just desserts of her own treachery—that is, Nahum itself *is* the call for revenge.

In collusion, Lamentations and Nahum invite their readers into the pathos of a city's destruction. Both describe this devastation as taken out on the body of a woman, apparently sharing the conviction that penetration/invasion is the worst thing that can happen to a woman—and to a city (see 'Nahum and [Wo]men').

B. Collision

1. *Daughter Nineveh?* Female personification takes slightly different forms in Nahum and in Lamentations, however. While Nineveh is called a whore, Jerusalem is called a widow (Lam. 1.2), a daughter (Lam. 1.6; 2.1, 2, 5, 8, 13), and a virgin daughter (Lam. 1.15; 2.13), labels that are amazingly non-accusatory in a book that repeatedly reminds the reader of Judah's guilt (Lam. 1.5, 8, 14, 18, 20, 22; 4.13). Lamentations' choice of vocabulary reminds the reader that Nahum could have assigned guilt to Nineveh without calling the city a *zônâ*; the label is clearly a slur, not a metaphor. Similarly, Lamentations' ability to mourn a sinful Jerusalem and to continue to call her a daughter (just as the OAN of Jer. 46–51 call foreign cities 'daughter') highlights Nahum's lack of compassion for the one who is justly punished. Nahum's refusal to demonstrate any concern

for the vanquished Nineveh, indeed, is an attempt to keep Nineveh totally Other, distant from the reader.

2. *What is uncovered?* On first comparison, the picture of the humiliation of Jerusalem in Lamentations seems less sexualized than that of Nineveh in Nahum. Nineveh's skirts are raised over her face and nations look on her shame (Nah. 3. 5), while Jerusalem's shame is described as 'filth' and 'uncleanness' (Lam. 1.8-9)—interpreted by many commentators as menstrual uncleanness, though both terms can refer to ritual uncleanness of different origins (e.g. Lev. 20, Num. 19).

An intertextual reading of Lamentations with Nahum, however, highlights possible sexual connotations in the language of Lamentations. As we have seen, the verbal root *gālâ* can be translated both as 'send to exile' and 'uncover', and the likely double-entendre of *gālâ* in Nah. 2.7 was explored in the commentary. In Lamentations, *gālâ* not only appears in 1.3, but also in Lam. 4.21-22—a passage that is rich in intertextual connections with Nahum: 'Rejoice and be glad, O daughter Edom, you that live in the land of Uz; but to you also the cup shall pass; you shall become drunk and strip yourself bare.' The punishment of your iniquity, O daughter Zion, is accomplished, he will keep you in exile no longer; but your iniquity, O daughter Edom, he will punish, he will uncover (*gillâ*) your sins.

This passage is noteworthy, first of all, because it links the daughter's self-stripping and Yahweh's uncovering of her sins, offering further verification that *gālâ* can bear a sexual connotation. Lamentations 4.21-22 becomes even more complex, however, when read in light of the discussion earlier in this chapter about 'stripping' in Nahum, Jeremiah 49, and Obadiah. The Lamentations text not only exhibits a striking juxtaposition of gender identities ('daughter Edom'), but also identifies the perpetrator of the stripping in a new way. In Nahum, Yahweh uncovers Nineveh; in Jeremiah 49, the male Esau is stripped (the verb is passive); and in Obadiah Esau is covered with shame, but Lamentations predicts that in her drunkenness daughter Edom will strip herself. Here, in a single phrase, the complications of Yahweh's agency (as in Nahum) and the anxiety of male exposure (as in Jeremiah) are averted, though, in the aftermath, Lamentations creates an hermaphroditic Edom, a male/female who strips himself/herself.

In an intertextual reading, the sexualized nature of Nineveh's assault spills over into Lamentations. The 'precious things' and 'sanctuary' of Lam. 1.10 ('Enemies have stretched out their hands over all her precious things; she has even seen the nations invade her sanctuary…'), like the 'hiding places' of Jer. 49.10, resonate differently when read alongside

Nah. 3.5 ('I...will lift up your skirts over your face; and I will let nations look on your nakedness and kingdoms on your shame').

In turn, reading Lamentations also highlights another passage in Nahum. In the course of describing the atrocities of the invading armies, Lam. 5.11 laments that 'women are raped in Zion, virgins in the towns of Judah'. The verb here used for 'rape' ('*innû*) is from the root '*anâ*, which figured prominently in my discussion of Nah. 1.12, where the NRSV translates '*anâ* as 'afflicted': 'Though I have afflicted you, I will afflict you no more'. Nahum reads quite differently when '*anâ* is given its other nuance: Yahweh proclaims, 'I have raped you. I will rape you no more'. Such a reading suggests that Nineveh is not the only female assaulted in Nahum; both Nineveh and Judah are females controlled by the all-powerful Yahweh. Judah is promised salvation not just from her treatment by the Assyrians but also from her treatment by her own very-male deity.

3. *Guilt*. As we have seen, neither Lamentations nor Nahum goes into detail about the vanquished city's crimes. Dwelling on the pathos of the situation, they acknowledge but do not explicate the reasons behind the city's punishment.

According to Cooper, this reticence to explain the fault of the vanquished is also a feature of Mespotamian city laments. The classic city laments, Cooper argues, fail to blame the city's inhabitants for its fate and 'place the responsibility for the loss of power and destruction of Sumerian cities squarely on the shoulders of the great gods and the divine assembly' (1983: 29). He highlights that even *The Curse of Agade*, which blames Naramsin for Agade's destruction, also attributes the city's fate to the unexplained turn in Inanna's (and Enlil's) affections.

Similarly, while in Lamentations Jerusalem calls for revenge against her enemies, she blames Yahweh for her plight. She admits that she has been rebellious but never specifies the nature of that rebellion.

A reading of Lamentations and the city laments calls attention to the laconic way in which Nahum has addressed Assyria's crimes. The book's opening theophany, for example, pays far more attention to the strength and power of Yahweh to crush his foes than to the precise criteria by which those foes are named. While a reader of the Hebrew Bible and a student of Assyrian texts easily can supply the details of Assyrian brutality, Nahum, surprisingly, only describes Nineveh's crimes in metaphorical and stereotypical terms. In the light of these intertexts, Nahum speaks far more about the ability of Yahweh to crush foes than about the crimes that offend Yahweh, and the free-floating pronouns of Nahum 1 ('you', 'they') become more clearly a deliberate strategy to keep enemies

vague and generic so that full attention remains on Yahweh's ability to
crush all foes.

4. *Voice.* Perhaps the greatest difference of all between Nahum and
Lamentations remains the perspective from which the text is narrated: in
Lamentations, the one who has been afflicted/raped speaks. While
Jerusalem is not the only voice in Lamentations (the poet speaks in 1.1-
11a and 2.1-19; Jerusalem in 1.11b-22 and 2.20-22, and elsewhere), the
reader of Lamentations consistently is encouraged to side *with* Jerusalem, to understand her catastrophe from her vantage point, to empathize with her, to experience her pain. Even the acknowledgment of
Jerusalem's guilt does not negate her right to complain, a dual reality
which Lam. 1.18 powerfully holds together: 'Yahweh is in the right, for I
have rebelled against his word; *but* hear, all you peoples, and behold my
suffering; my young women and young men have gone into captivity.'

In contrast to those who discern the core of Lamentations in the
expression of hope in ch. 3, Linafelt (2002) locates the 'voice' of the
book in its anguish and outpouring of grief, especially that of Jerusalem
herself. He deems Lamentations 'survival literature', akin to the accounts
of Holocaust survivors, which insists that pain must be witnessed.

While in Lamentations the Self fervently and repeatedly mourns its
punishment, Nahum denies the Other the same right. Nahum grants
Nineveh neither voice nor sympathy. The guilty one is seen only from
the stance of the narrator, which in the superscription is equated with
the stance of Yahweh. None of the pathos of Nahum is expressed from
the standpoint of the vanquished.

Attention to voice also reveals that in the narrative world of Nahum
Judah is as voiceless as Nineveh. Nahum/Yahweh speaks *to* Judah, but
the reader hears neither Judah's own sense of pain nor whether Judah
accepts Nahum's assumption that Nineveh's punishment alleviates her
own. The multiple voices that speak in the city laments and in Lamentations are absent from Nahum. Neither Nineveh nor Judah are given
voice.

5. *Children.* In Lamentations, Jerusalem protests not only her own fate
but that of her children. Of all the victims of war, Lamentations pays the
greatest attention to them:

> My eyes are spent with weeping; my stomach churns; my bile is poured out
> on the ground because of the destruction of my people, because infants
> and babes faint in the streets of the city. They cry to their mothers, 'Where
> is bread and wine?' as they faint like the wounded in the streets of the city,
> as their life is poured out on their mothers' bosom (2.11-12).

> Arise, cry out in the night, at the beginning of the watches! Pour out your heart like water before the presence of the Lord! Lift your hands to him for the lives of your children, who faint for hunger at the head of every street (2.19).

> The tongue of the infant sticks to the roof of its mouth for thirst; the children beg for food, but no one gives them anything (4.4).

Indeed, as Linafelt (2000: 50) underscores, in Lamentations 'the laments of both Zion and the poet culminate in a concern for the lives of children who are dying in the streets'.

What about Nineveh's children? Nahum's only intimation that infants die in war is the brief comment that the infants of Thebes were smashed in pieces at the head of every street (3.10). In contrast to Lamentations, Nahum never mentions the hunger or slaughter of children in war; nothing in Nahum corresponds to the plea in Lamentations for Yahweh to heed the cries of suffering children. Lamentations's insistent call for Yahweh to have pity on the children reminds us of Nahum's 'erasure', its unsuccessful attempt to hide the reality of the suffering of Assyrian children by failing to mention them.

6. *The Lamentations of Nineveh.* Intertextual readings are subversive, because they blur the boundaries between 'us' and 'them'. They let characters switch roles, and they listen for how the production changes as a result. In the case of Lamentations and Nineveh, they ponder what would happen if each read the other's part.

How would Lamentations sound if it were spoken by Nineveh–if that city, rather than Jerusalem, spoke?

Nineveh's Lament (adapted from the NRSV translation of Lamentations)	*resonances in Nahum*
How lonely sits the city that once was full of people! How like a widow she has become, she that was great among the nations! She that was a princess among the provinces has become a vassal. She weeps bitterly in the night, with tears on her cheeks; among all her lovers she has no one to comfort her; all her friends have dealt treacherously with her, they have become her enemies... Her foes have become the masters, her enemies prosper, because Yahweh has made her suffer for the multitude of her transgressions; her children have gone away, captives before the foe... Nineveh sinned grievously, so she has become a mockery; all who honored her despise her, for they have seen her nakedness; she herself groans, and turns her face away... with none to comfort her. 'O Yahweh, look at my affliction, for the enemy has triumphed!'	cf. Nah. 3.4: Nineveh as *zônâ* 'lovers' implied by the usage of *zônâ*? Nah. 3.7: no comforters Nah. 3.4: multitude of harlotries Nah. 3.10: children of Thebes Nah. 3.5: nakedness Nah. 3.7: no comforters

Look and see if there is any sorrow like my sorrow, which was brought upon me, which Yahweh inflicted on the day of his fierce anger… Yahweh has rejected all my warriors in the midst of me; he proclaimed a time against me to crush my young men… Yahweh is in the right, for I have rebelled against his word; but hear, all you peoples, and behold my suffering; my young women and young men have gone into captivity… All my enemies heard of my trouble; they are glad that you have done it. Bring on the day you have announced, and let them be as I am. Let all their evil doing come before you; and deal with them as you have dealt with me because of all my transgressions; for my groans are many and my heart is faint… My eyes are spent with weeping; my stomach churns; my bile is poured out on the ground because of the destruction of my people, because infants and babes faint in the streets of the city. They cry to their mothers, 'Where is bread and wine?' as they faint like the wounded in the streets of the city, as their life is poured out on their mothers' bosom…' All your enemies open their mouths against you; they hiss, they gnash their teeth, they cry: 'We have devoured her! Ah, this is the day we longed for; at last we have seen it!'… Should women eat their offspring, the children they have borne?… The young and the old are lying on the ground in the streets; my young women and my young men have fallen by the sword; in the day of your anger you have killed them, slaughtering without mercy. You invited my enemies from all around as if for a day of festival; and on the day of the anger of Yahweh no one escaped or survived.	Nah. 1.2-3: Yahweh's anger Nah. 2 and 3: fall of Assyrian warriors Nah. 3.10: exile Nah. 2.11: hearts melt… Nah. 3.5-7: enemies watch Nah. 3.3: piles of dead Nah. 1.2-3: Yahweh's anger

In entertaining such a reading, I do not intend to equate Nineveh with Jerusalem. But I do intend to let this heuristic draw attention to the rhetorical and ideological strategies of Nahum—how, in comparison to its alter ego Lamentations, it silences and demonizes Nineveh. Lamentations gives voice to all that Nahum leaves unsaid about war and about the possibility that Yahweh's punishment might be overly harsh.

The role switching invited by intertextual readings also allows the possibility of a *maśśā'* against Judah, a Nahum spoken against Judah rather than an external foe. Such a reading fills fewer gaps, however, for Nahum reread as diatribe against Judah sounds like much of the prophetic literature. Elsewhere, Judah is described as under siege and called a *zônâ*. Within the Hebrew Bible, Judah is punished like the nations but, unlike them, she is allowed to protest her fate.

V. Conclusion

According to Ellen van Wolde (1989: 47), intertextuality is the concern, and perhaps also the creation, of the reader:

> in an intertextual analysis or interpretation of a text it is the reader and not the writer who is centre of attention, because it is the reader who makes a text interfere with the other text. The writer assigns meaning to his own context and in interaction with other texts he shapes and forms his own text. The reader, in much the same way, assigns meaning to the generated text in interaction with other texts he knows. Without a reader a text is only a lifeless collection of words.

While throughout this volume I have talked in general terms about Nahum's reader, in the final analysis *I* am the reader who has interacted with Nahum's rhetorical world, who has placed alongside Nahum selected intertexts, and who has asked of Nahum the questions that matter most to me. Obviously, I have created the readings in this chapter by choosing to read Lamentations as a final intertext to Nahum.

That choice arises from my choice to read with the suffering, a perspective I attempted to explain in the Introduction. But such a reading strategy is complicated by how many suffer in Nahum—Nineveh suffers, Judah suffers, Thebes suffers, children suffer—and by Nahum's insistence that the suffering of one is necessary to the salvation of another. For Nahum, Nineveh's suffering signals a cessation to Judah's suffering.

Through various rhetorical strategies, Nahum attempts to portray Nineveh's suffering as something in which to rejoice. In the cumulative logic of the book, Nineveh is equated with Yahweh's enemy, the one from whose endless cruelty no one has escaped. By denying voice to Nineveh and by ignoring her children, Nahum attempts to preclude sympathy for Nineveh's fate. There for me lies the rub of Nahum. I find it difficult to witness suffering without responding with sympathy—even for the guilty.

The faint contours of the faces of children and women that materialize on the fuzzy boundaries of Nahum's text destabilize for me its casting of Nineveh as a monolithic, faceless Other. I keep losing sight of who is 'us' and who is 'them', and I keep forgetting that the questions Lamentations and Nahum ask are intended to be rhetorical. When Jerusalem asks, 'Is there any sorrow like my sorrow, which Yahweh has done to me, which Yahweh did in his anger?' (Lam. 1.12), I catch myself thinking about Nineveh and Thebes, Mozambique, Auschwitz, and Deir Yassin; and when Nahum queries, 'Nineveh is devastated; who will bemoan her?' (Nah. 3.7), I involuntarily reply, 'I will mourn her—and Jerusalem, too'. With all those faces bleeding through the white surface of the text, I keep forgetting whose pain I am supposed to ignore.

In my own moral calculus, such forgetfulness does not negate the suffering of the victim; it does not equate the pain of the oppressor with that of the oppressed. Rather, building into my own awareness the humanity of the oppressor is the best hedge I know against the risk of the ideological blindness that feeds the cycle of atrocity—the perpetual creation of a yet another faceless Other, ripe for annihilation.

Nineveh was a brutal oppressor, a fierce predator. But as the Assyrian reliefs so clearly show (see Plate 12), one can appreciate the agony and pathos of the dying lioness without ignoring her power to destroy.

Postscript

The manuscript of this book was completed in the summer of 2001. When I wrote here about the ideologies of retaliatory violence, I had no way of imagining the terrorist attacks in the United States on 11 September 2001, and their aftermath.

As I reread my work from the vantage point of the autumn of 2001, not knowing what might yet transpire before this volume reaches publication, I find that I believe what I have written here more than ever before. In the media that has filled the last month, I have seen and heard in the public arena, just as I did in text of Nahum, how the demonization of the Other feeds the cycle of violence. The enemy is rendered fit for annihilation *both* by al-Qaeda's refusal to acknowledge the humanity of its victims *and also* the American insistence on labeling terrorists as cowards rather than as persons of deep ideological conviction.

But also around me are those who, even now in the contemporary scene, are naming just how false are the dichotomies between 'us' and 'them' and who are keeping human the faces of those marked as Other. For them I am grateful, and to their efforts I contribute my own voice and vision.

Julia Myers O'Brien
11 October 2001

Bibliography

Aberbach, D.

    1993   *Imperialism and Biblical Prophecy, 750–500 BCE* (New York: Routledge).

Achtemeier, E.

    1986   *Nahum–Malachi* (Interpretation; Atlanta: John Knox Press).

Ball, E.

    1999   '"When the Towers Fall": Interpreting Nahum as Christian Scripture', in E. Ball (ed.), *In Search of True Wisdom* (JSOTSup, 300; Sheffield: Sheffield Academic Press): 211-30.

Beal, T.

    1992a   'Glossary', in Fewell 1992: 21-24.

    1992b   'Ideology and Intertextuality: Surplus of Meaning and Controlling the Means of Production', in Fewell 1992: 27-39.

    1997   *The Book of Hiding: Gender, Ethnicity, Annihilation and Esther* (New York: Routledge).

Ben Zvi, E.

    1991   *A Historical-Critical Study of the Book of Zephaniah* (BZAW, 198; Berlin: W. de Gruyter).

    1996   'Studying Prophetic Texts against their Original Backgrounds: Pre-Ordained Scripts and Alternative Horizons of Research', in S.B. Reid (ed.), *Prophets and Paradigms: Essays in Honor of Gene Tucker* (JSOTSup, 229; Sheffield: Sheffield Academic Press): 125-35.

Bersani, L., and U. Dutoit

    1985   *The Forms of Violence: Narrative in Assyrian Art and Modern Culture* (New York: Schocken Books).

Bird, P.

    1989   '"To Play the Harlot": An Inquiry Into an Old Testament Metaphor', in P.L. Day (ed.), *Gender and Difference in Ancient Israel* (Minneapolis: Augsburg–Fortress): 75-94.

Boer, P.A.H. de

    1948   'An Inquiry into the Meaning of the Term *maśśā*'', *OTS* 5: 197-214.

Brenner, A. (ed.)

    1995   *A Feminist Companion to the Latter Prophets* (FCB, 8; Sheffield: Sheffield Academic Press).

Brownmiller, S.

    1975   *Against Our Will: Men, Women and Rape* (Toronto: Bantam).

Burlein, A.

    2002   *Lift High the Cross: Where White Supremacy and the Religious Right Converge* (Durham, NC: Duke University Press).

Butler, J.

    1990   *Gender Trouble: Feminism and the Subversion of Identity* (London: Routledge).

| | 1993 | *Bodies that Matter: On the Discursive Limits of 'Sex'* (London: Routledge). |

Calkins, R.
1947   *The Modern Message of the Modern Prophets* (New York: Harper & Bros).

Camus, A.
1961   *Resistance, Rebellion, and Death* (New York: Alfred A. Knopf).

Carroll, R.
1983   'Poets not Prophets', *JSOT* 27: 25-31.
1986   *Jeremiah* (OTL; London: SCM Press).
1988   'Inventing the Prophets, Essay in Honour of Professor Jacob Weingreen to be Presented on the Occasion of his 80th Birthday', *IBS* 10: 24-36.

Cathcart, K J.
1992   'Nahum', in *ABD*: IV, 998-1000.
1973   *Nahum in the Light of Northwest Semitic* (BibOr, 26; Rome: Biblical Institute Press).

Charles, J.D.
1989   'Plundering the Lion's Den—A Portrait of Divine Fury (Nahum 2.3-11)', *GTJ* 10.2: 183-201.

Chase, M.E.
1952   *The Bible and the Common Reader* (New York: Macmillan, rev. edn 1st edn 1945).

Christensen, D.L.
1975   'The Acrostic of Nahum Reconsidered', *ZAW* 87: 17-30.
1988   'Nahum', in *HBC*: 736-38.
1999   'Nahum, book of', in *DBI*: II, 199-201.

Cleland, J.
1956   'Exposition' on 'Nahum', in *IB*: VI, 957-69.

Coggins, R.
1982   'An Alternative Prophetic Tradition?', in R. Coggins, A. Phillips, and M. Knibb (eds.), *Israel's Prophetic Tradition: Essays in Honour of Peter R. Ackroyd* (Cambridge: Cambridge University Press): 77-94.
1985   *Israel Among the Nations: Nahum, Obadiah, Esther* (ITC; Grand Rapids: Eerdmans).

Collins, T.
1993   *The Mantle of Elijah: The Redaction Criticism of the Prophetical Books* (BibSem; Sheffield: JSOT Press).

Cooper, J.S.
1983   *The Curse of Agade* (Baltimore: The Johns Hopkins University Press).

Craigie, P.
1985   *Twelve Prophets*, II (The Daily Study Bible Series; Philadelphia: Westminster Press).

Dobbs-Allsopp, F.W.
1993   *Weep, O Daughter of Jerusalem: A Study of the City-Lament Genre in the Hebrew Bible* (BibOr, 44; Rome: Biblical Institute Press).

Ellis, M.
  1997   *Unholy Alliance: Religion and Atrocity in Our Time* (Minneapolis: Fortress Press).
Erlandsson, S.
  1970   *The Burden of Babylon: A Study of Isaiah 13.2–14.23* (ConBOT, 4; Lund: C.W.K. Gleerup).
Evans, D.
  1980   'If Poets Must Have Flags', in Feinberg 1980: 20-21.
Exum, C.
  1995   'The Ethics of Biblical Violence against Women', in J.W. Rogerson, M. Davies, and M.D. Carroll R. (eds.), *The Bible in Ethics: The Second Sheffield Colloquium* (JSOTSup, 207; Sheffield: Sheffield Academic Press): 248-71.
Feinberg, B. (ed.)
  1980   *Poets to the People: South African Freedom Poems* (London: Heinemann).
Fewell, D. (ed.),
  1992   *Reading Between Texts: Intertextuality and the Hebrew Bible* (Louisville, KY: Westminster/John Knox Press).
Floyd, M.
  1994   'The Chimeral Acrostic of Nahum 1.2-10', *JBL* 113: 421-37.
  2000   *Minor Prophets. Part 2*. Vol XXII. (FOTL, 22; Grand Rapids: Eerdmans).
Fontaine, C.R.
  1997   'The Abusive Bible: On the Use of Feminist Method in Pastoral Contexts', in A. Brenner and C. Fontaine (eds.), *A Feminist Companion to Reading the Bible: Approaches, Strategies, Methods* (FCB, 11; Sheffield: Sheffield Academic Press): 84-113.
Fowl, S.
  1998   *Engaging Scripture: A Model for Theological Interpretation* (Malden, MA: Basil Blackwell).
  1995   'Texts Don't Have Ideologies', *BibInt* 3: 15-34.
Fox, M.
  1980   'The Rhetoric of Ezekiel's Vision of the Valley of the Bones', *HUCA* 51: 1-15.
García-Treto, F.
  1996   'Nahum', in *NIB*: VII, 591-619.
Gordon, P., and H.C. Washington
  1995   'Rape as a Military Metaphor in the Hebrew Bible', in Brenner 1995: 308-25.
Grayson, A.K.
  1992   'Mesopotamia, history of (Assyria)', in *ABD*: IV, 732-55.
Harlow, B.
  1987   *Resistance Literature* (New York: Methuen).
Heschel, A.J.
  1962   *The Prophets* (New York: Harper & Row).

Hillers, D.
    1964   *Treaty Curses and the Old Testament Prophets* (BibOr 16; Rome: Pontifical Biblical Institute).

Hilprecht, H.V.
    1903   *Explorations in Bible Lands During the 19th Century* (Philadelphia: A.J. Homan & Co.).

Holloway, S.W.
    2000   'Biblical Assyria and Other Anxieties in the British Empire' (Paper delivered at SBL Annual Meeting, Nashville, TN, 18–21 November).

Hutcheon, L.
    1989   *The Politics of Postmodernism* (New York: Routledge).

Iser, W.
    1978   *The Act of Reading: A Theory of Aesthetic Response* (Baltimore, MD: The Johns Hopkins University Press).

Jones, B.
    1996   *Howling over Moab: Irony and Rhetoric in Isaiah 15–16* (SBLDS, 157; Atlanta: Scholars Press).

Kermode, F.
    1979   *The Genesis of Secrecy: On the Interpretation of Narrative* (Cambridge, MA: Harvard University Press).

Kramer, S.N.
    1949   *Lament over the Destruction of Ur* (Chicago: University of Chicago Press).

Kumalo, A.N.C.
    1980   'Red our Colour', in Feinberg 1980: 58.

Levinas, E.
    1961   *Totality and Infinity: An Essay in Exteriority* (trans. A. Lingis; Pittsburgh: Duquesne University Press).

Linafelt, T.
    2000   *Surviving Lamentations: Catastrophe, Lament, and Protest in the Afterlife of a Biblical Book* (Chicago: University of Chicago Press).

Lipiński, E.
    1971   'Nahum', in *EncJud*: XII, 793-95.

Magdalene, F.R.
    1995   'Ancient Near Eastern Treaty Curses and the Ultimate Texts of Terror: A Study of the Language of Divine Sexual Abuse in the Prophetic Corpus', in Brenner 1995: 326-52.

Marks, H.
    1987   'The Twelve Prophets', in R. Alter and F. Kermode (eds.), *The Literary Guide to the Bible* (Cambridge, MA: Belknap Press of Harvard University Press): 207-33.

Mason, R.
    1991   *Micah, Nahum, Obadiah* (OTG, 28; Sheffield: JSOT Press).

Miscall, P.
    1992   'Isaiah: New Heavens, New Earth, New Book', in Fewell 1992: 41-56.

Moore, S.D.
    1989   *Literary Criticism and the Gospels: The Theoretical Challenge* (New Haven: Yale University Press).

Morrison, T.
    1992   *Playing in the Dark* (Cambridge, MA: Harvard University Press).
Nogalski, J.
    1993a   *Literary Precursors of the Book of the Twelve* (BZAW, 217; Berlin:
               W. de Gruyter).
    1993b   *Redactional Processes in the Book of the Twelve* (BZAW, 218; Berlin:
               W. de Gruyter).
Nussbaum, M.
    1990   *Love's Knowledge: Essays on Philosophy and Literature* (Oxford:
               Oxford University Press).
Orelli, C. von
    1893   *The Twelve Minor Prophets* (trans. J.S. Banks; Edinburgh: T. & T.
               Clark).
Pardes, I.
    1992   *Countertraditions in the Bible: A Feminist Approach* (Cambridge,
               MA: Harvard University Press).
Patterson, R.D., and M.E. Travers,
    1990   'Nahum: Poet Laureate of the Minor Prophets', *JETS* 33: 437-44.
Peckham, B.
    1993   *History and Prophecy: The Development of Late Judean Literary
               Traditions* (New York: Doubleday).
Peels, H.G.L.
    1995   *The Vengeance of God: The Meaning of the Root NQM and the
               Function of the NQM-Texts in the Context of Divine Revelation in the
               Old Testament* (Leiden: E.J. Brill).
Pitard, W.T.
    1992   'Vengeance', in *ABD*: VI, 786-87.
Portmann, J.
    2000   *When Bad Things Happen to Other People* (New York: Routledge).
Preminger, A., and E.L. Greenstein (eds.)
    1986   *The Hebrew Bible in Literary Criticism* (New York: Ungar).
Rad, G. von
    1965   *Old Testament Theology*, II (trans. D.M.G. Stalker; New York: Harper
               & Row).
    1967   *The Message of the Prophets* (trans. D.M.G. Stalker; New York: Harper
               & Row).
Richlin, A.
    1992   'Reading Ovid's Rapes', in *Pornography and Representation in
               Greece and Rome* (New York: Oxford University Press).
Roberts, J.J.M.
    1991   *Nahum, Habakkuk, and Zephaniah: A Commentary* (OTL; Louisville,
               KY: Westminster/John Knox Press).
Robinson, C.L.
    1952   *The Twelve Minor Prophets* (Grand Rapids: Baker Book House).
Roux, G.
    1980   *Ancient Iraq* (Harmondsworth: Penguin Books, 2nd edn).

Rowlett, L.
  1996   *Joshua and the Rhetoric of Violence: A New Historicist Analysis* (JSOTSup, 226; Sheffield: Sheffield Academic Press).
Saggs, H.W.
  1965   *Everyday Life in Babylonia and Assyria* (London: Batsford; New York: G.P. Putnam's Sons).
Said, E.
  1979   *Orientalism* (New York: Vintage Books).
  1985   *Beginnings: Intention and Method* (repr.; New York: Columbia University Press).
Sanderson, J.E.
  1992   'Nahum', in C.A. Newsom and S.H. Ringe (eds.), *The Women's Bible Commentary* (London: SPCK; Louisville, KY: Westminster/John Knox Press): 217-21.
Scott, J.C.
  1990   *Domination and the Arts of Resistance: Hidden Transcripts* (New Haven: Yale University Press).
Searight, S.
  1979   *The British in the Middle East* (London and the Hague: East–West Publications).
Smith, G.A.
  1903   'Nahum', in *The Expositor's Bible* (New York: A.C. Armstrong & Son).
Smith, J.M.P.
  1911   'Nahum', in J.M.P. Smith, W.H. Ward, and J.A. Brewer (eds.), *A Critical and Exegetical Commentary on Micah, Zephaniah, Nahum, Habakkuk, Obadiah, and Joel* (ICC; New York: Charles Scribner's Sons).
Smith, R.L.
  1984   *Micah–Malachi* (WBC, 32; Waco, TX: Word Books).
Spronk, K.
  1997   *Nahum* (Kampen: Kok Pharos).
Stout, J.
  1982   'What is the Meaning of a Text?', *New Literary History* 14: 1-12.
Sweeney, M.
  1992   'Concerning the Structure and Generic Character of the Book of Nahum', *ZAW* 194: 364-77.
Thistlethwaite, S.
  1993   '"May You Enjoy the Spoil of Your Enemies": Rape as a Biblical Metaphor for War', in *Semeia* 61: C. Camp and C. Fontaine, *Women, War, and Metaphor: Language and Society in the Study of the Hebrew Bible*: 59-75.
Tolbert, M.A.
  1989   *Sowing the Gospel: Mark's World in Literary-Historical Perspective* (Minneapolis: Augsburg–Fortress).
Tucker, G.
  1977   'Prophetic Superscriptions and the Growth of a Canon', in G.W. Coats and B.O. Long (eds.), *Canon and Authority: Essays in Old*

Testament Religion and Theology (Philadelphia: Fortress Press): 56-70.

Vries, S.J. de
1966   'The Acrostic of Nahum in the Jerusalem Liturgy', *VT* 16: 476-81.

Wendland, E.R.
1998   'What's the "Good News"? Check out "the feet"! Prophetic Rhetoric and the Salvific Centre of Nahum's Vision', *OTE* 11.1: 154-81.

Wessels, W.
1998   'Nahum: An Uneasy Expression of Yahweh's Power', *OTE* 11.3: 615-28.

Winter, I.J.
1981   'Royal Rhetoric and the Development of Historical Narrative in Neo-Assyrian Reliefs', *Studies in Visual Communication* 7.2: 2-38.

Wolde, E. van
1989   'Trendy Intertextuality?', in S. Draisma (ed.), *Intertextuality in Biblical Writings: Essays in Honour of Bas van Iersel* (Kampen: J.H. Kok): 43-49.

Woude, A.S. van der
1977   'The Book of Nahum: A Letter Written in Exile', *OTS* 20: 108-26.

INDEXES

INDEX OF REFERENCES

OLD TESTAMENT

Readings Supplement Series

Graham Ogden, *Qoheleth* (1987)
Margaret Davies, *Matthew* (1993)
Peter D. Miscall, *Isaiah* (1993)
Mark W.G. Stibbe, *John* (1993)
Francis Landy, *Hosea* (1995)
F. Scott Spencer, *Acts* (1997)
Norman Whybray, *Job* (1998)
Edgar W. Conrad, *Zechariah* (1999)
Jonathan Knight, *Revelation* (1999)
Jerry W. McCant, *2 Corinthians* (1999)
Robert P. Gordon, *Hebrews* (2000)
Laurence A. Turner, *Genesis* (2000)
Edwin K. Broadhead, *Mark* (2001)
Julia Myers O'Brien, *Nahum* (2002)